Simple networking
with Windows 98

Other Books of Interest

Simple networking with Windows 98

Jim Gatenby

BERNARD BABANI (publishing) LTD
The Grampians
Shepherds Bush Road
London W6 7NF
England

Please Note

Although every care has been taken with the production of this book to ensure that any projects, designs, modifications and/or programs, etc., contained herewith, operate in a correct and safe manner and also that any components specified are normally available in Great Britain, the Publishers and Author do not accept responsibility in any way for the failure (including fault in design) of any project, design, modification or program to work correctly or to cause damage to any equipment that it may be connected to or used in conjunction with, or in respect of any other damage or injury that may be so caused, nor do the Publishers accept responsibility in any way for the failure to obtain specified components.

Notice is also given that if equipment that is still under warranty is modified in any way or used or connected with home-built equipment then that warranty may be void.

First Published - December1999

British Library Cataloguing in Publication Data:

A catalogue record for this book is available from the
British Library

ISBN 0 85934 469 X

Cover Design by Gregor Arthur
Cover illustration by Adam Willis
Printed and bound in Great Britain by The Bath Press, Bath

About this Book

Creating a small network is now a very worthwhile enterprise for anyone with more than one computer, providing a cost-effective way to manage information and share expensive hardware. The purpose of this book is to introduce the reader to the concepts of networking and to show how simple but effective small networks, which bring real advantages, can be created.

Although previously the exclusive domain of the technical specialist in large organisations, recent developments have brought networking technology within the reach of the ordinary user:

- All of the necessary networking software is available free as part of Windows 98 (and Windows 95). Perhaps more importantly, it's easy to install and configure.

- Hardware kits are now obtainable at a modest price, containing everything you need to network two or more machines. It's a simple task to assemble the network and then manage it using the tools provided in Windows 98, such as the Network Neighborhood and Net Watcher.

Many homes now have two (and sometimes more) computers and there are lots of small concerns, offices and groups such as primary schools with a cluster of machines. Substantial benefits can be derived by creating a simple "peer-to-peer" network which links the machines together:

- Several users can share the same applications software and information files.

- File transfer between computers is much more efficient than alternative copying methods such as disc swapping.

- Expensive devices such as printers and scanners can be shared by several computers across the network with no appreciable loss in performance.

- A single Internet connection using only one modem and telephone line can be shared simultaneously by several networked computers.

The first chapter of the book describes the simplest network of all - created by connecting two machines with just a cheap cable linking their serial, parallel or USB ports. This is useful for copying files between any two computers such as say, a laptop used out on the road and an office-based desktop machine. This simple network can be managed by the Direct Cable Connection (a component of Windows 98) and by third party software such as Traveling LapLink Professional described in more detail in the last chapter. (Some of the tasks involved in setting up the Direct Cable Connection are also involved when configuring a peer-to-peer network as described later in the book. For the convenience of the reader, these common topics are duplicated so that each part of the book is free-standing.) The latest ultra fast USB technology is also discussed and instructions are given (in the Appendix) for installing additional USB and parallel ports.

Full-blown networks are introduced in Chapter 2 and the powerful client/server model used in large organisations is compared with the peer-to-peer network used in small concerns. Subsequent chapters discuss the hardware components needed for an Ethernet network, the prevailing standard. This is followed by guidance on the building and management of a small peer-to-peer system.

Later chapters discuss sharing a single Internet connection between several networked computers using third party software as well as Windows 98 Internet Connection Sharing, part of Windows 98 Second Edition.

The last chapter discusses Traveling LapLink Professional, which apart from many enhanced features for copying files between networked computers, also contains facilities for communication, controlling a remote computer and printing at both ends of a network link between two computers.

Although prepared using Windows 98, much of the material in this book should also be relevant to Windows 95 users.

About the Author

Jim Gatenby trained as a Chartered Mechanical Engineer and initially worked at Rolls-Royce Ltd using mainframe computers in the analysis of gas turbine performance. He obtained a Master of Philosophy degree in Mathematical Education by research at Loughborough University of Technology and has taught mathematics and computing to 'A' Level since 1972. His most recent posts have included Head of Computer Studies and Network Manager. During this time he has written several books in the field of educational computing and Microsoft Windows.

Trademarks

Microsoft, Windows and Outlook Express are trademarks or registered trademarks of Microsoft Corporation. Traveling Software and LapLink are trademarks or registered trademarks of LapLink Software, Inc. Symantec and pcANYWHERE are trademarks of Symantec Corporation. 3Com and OfficeConnect are registered trademarks of 3Com Corporation. i.Share and ModemShare are trademarks of Artisoft, Inc. PKZIP and PKUNZIP are registered trademarks of PKWARE,Inc. WinZip is a registered trademark of Nico Mak Computing, Inc.

All other brand and product names are recognised as trademarks, or registered trademarks, of their respective companies.

Acknowledgements

I would like to thank Traveling Software for providing me with a copy of their latest LapLink Professional software and data cable. Also Paul Bonathan at Artisoft Technical Support for help with Artisoft i.Share 3.0.

Contents

9

Simple Cable Connections

Introduction

The simplest of networks is formed when two computers are connected by a single short cable costing only a few pounds. A typical use for this rudimentary network is to copy files from a laptop to a desktop computer or from an old machine to its new replacement. Or to make backup copies of important files onto another machine; or to share one printer between two computers.

This simple network will lack the speed and sophistication of a more expensive arrangement such as the peer-to-peer and client/server networks discussed in the chapters which follow. However, since it requires none of the network components such as network interface cards and hubs it is an extremely cheap method of connecting two machines in order to share resources such as files and printers. Windows 98 contains all of the software to operate this simple network so the system can be up and running for the cost of the cable and a few minutes work.

The Windows 98 software provided for this task is the Direct Cable Connection and this chapter describes how to install the program from your Windows 98 CD and then how to set up and use the connection. Third party software packages such as Traveling LapLink and Symantec's pcANYWHERE can also be used for this purpose. Against the cost of buying these packages must be considered their enhanced facilities for copying files and additional features for use with local and wide area networks. The third party packages usually include a suitable data transfer cable. Traveling LapLink Professional is described in detail later in this book.

The Cable

It's essential to obtain the correct cable when setting up the **Direct Cable Connection**. Third party packages like Traveling LapLink Professional and pcANYWHERE usually include a free cable in the box but with Direct Cable Connection you'll need to buy one from a local dealer or by mail order.

Direct Cable Connection can either use a cable connecting the *serial ports* on the two computers or one connecting the *parallel ports*. The serial ports are the 9 or 25-way connectors on the back of the computer into which you normally plug a mouse or modem. The parallel port (often referred to as LPT1) is the connector normally used for the printer and other devices.

The speed of data transfers over a parallel cable is several times faster than over a serial cable.

When buying a cable it must be stressed that a *data transfer* cable is required. In the case of a serial cable it must be a *null-modem* i.e. non-modem cable, also known as a *cross-over* cable. The parallel cable must be either a *parallel link* or *LapLink* cable.

An ordinary printer cable will not work with two way data transfer programs like Direct Cable Connection or LapLink Professional.

The Maplin Electronics   catalogue (obtainable from W.H.Smith's) contains a good range of serial and parallel cables clearly described as suitable for data transfer.

http://www.maplin.co.uk.

Extra Ports

As mentioned earlier, the serial ports (COM1, COM2, etc.) are often used for mice and modems. It's possible to buy serial data cables with both 9-way and 25-way connectors at each end so that you can utilise both types of port on each of the computers to be connected. The parallel port (LPT1) is normally used for a printer and may also be used for a Zip drive or scanner. In many cases there is a socket for the printer on the back of the scanner or Zip drive but these sharing arrangements can cause problems. If you want to use the parallel port connection regularly for data transfer work, you will have the inconvenience of having to unplug devices such as printers, scanners and Zip drives. The answer is to fit an expansion card containing extra parallel ports. These can be bought for under £20 and are easy to fit. Expansion cards containing one or two parallel ports or a mixture of serial and parallel ports are available. This topic is covered in more detail in **Appendix B: Fitting a Parallel Port Expansion Card**.

USB

At the time of writing, new machines are supplied with the latest USB (Universal Serial Bus) ports. USB makes the setting up of new devices much simpler with genuine "plug and play" capability. You can attach a 4-port hub to the USB port on the back of your computer. Then further hubs can be connected to the first and subsequent hubs so that, in theory, by stacking the hubs, up to 127 peripheral devices can be connected. USB also provides "hot swapping" - the installation of new devices while the computer is running - there's no need to switch off or experiment with complex settings.

In the context of this chapter, however, USB technology can be used to provide extremely fast data transfers (several times faster than a parallel connection) over a short USB cable linking two adjacent computers.

Programs like LapLink Professional already support USB and the technology promises to become the standard for connecting new devices and for linking computers in the future. If you have a new Pentium machine, it will probably already be fitted with USB ports. Older Pentiums can be modified fairly cheaply but if you are not happy to remove the cover of your machine and "tinker" with your machine it should be possible to have the work done locally by a computer repair shop. **Appendix A: The Universal Serial Bus** describes how to check whether your machine supports USB and the upgrading of a computer by fitting any necessary components.

The Direct Cable Connection

Windows 98 provides its own program for connecting two computers by a short cable. At the time of writing, the **Direct Cable Connection** supports serial and parallel cables and the infra red connection provided on some laptop computers. The parallel data cable is currently the best option for the DCC but as discussed in the previous section it's essential to get a cable of the correct specification. Letters in the computer press have frequently referred to the complexity of setting up the DCC but provided you install all of the necessary Windows 98 components (discussed shortly), I have found it to be straightforward and reliable. It does however, lack some of the ease of use and additional features of third party data transfer packages such as pcANYWHERE and LapLink Professional. (The latter is discussed in detail later in this book).

Although DCC is provided free on the Windows 98 CD, it may not be installed on your computer. You can check by selecting **Start**, **Programs**, **Accessories** and **Communications**.

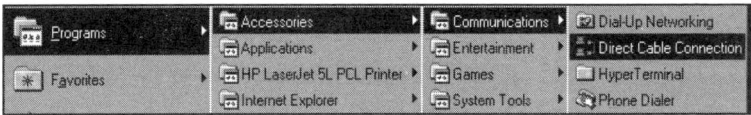

If the **Direct Cable Con-nection** doesn't appear on the list then the program must be installed from your Windows 98 CD. First select **Start**, **Settings**, **Control Panel**, and **Add/Remove Programs**.

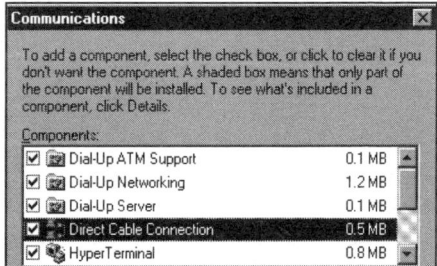

Then choose the **Windows Setup** tab and **Communications**. Now click **Details...**, make sure there's a tick on the box next to the **Direct Cable Connection** and then click **OK**. You will then be asked to insert the Windows 98 CD to complete the installation.

Essential Windows 98 Components

Before you attempt to run the Direct Cable Connection you need to ensure that a number of Windows 98 networking components are installed on each of the computers. Examine these in the **Network Configuration** tab (**Start, Settings, Control Panel, Network.**)

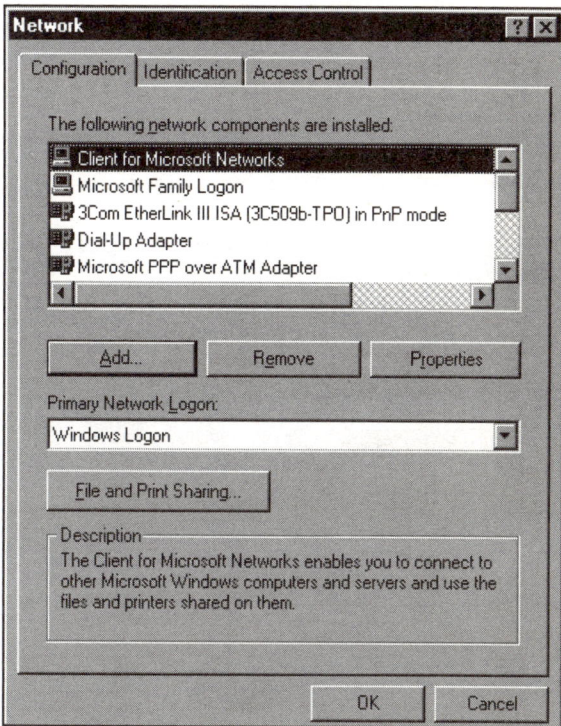

The components which must be present for DCC to work are :

- **IPX/SPX** - A network protocol or language
- **Client for Microsoft Networks**
- **File and Printer Sharing for Microsoft Networks**

Any components which are missing can be installed after clicking the **Add...** button. You will need to have your Windows 98 CD to hand.

Client for Microsoft Networks is reached by clicking **Add...** then **Client** then **Add...** and then selecting **Microsoft**. If you now select **Client for Microsoft Networks** and **OK** you will be asked for the Windows 98 CD so that the component can be installed.

IPX/SPX is installed in a similar manner. Select **Add...** then **Protocol** then **Add...** then **Microsoft** then **IPX/SPX-compatible Protocol**.

File and printer sharing for Microsoft Networks is installed after selecting **Add...** and **Service**.

While the main **Network Configuration** window is displayed you can give permission for other people to share your files and printer. This is done by clicking the **File and Print Sharing:** button.

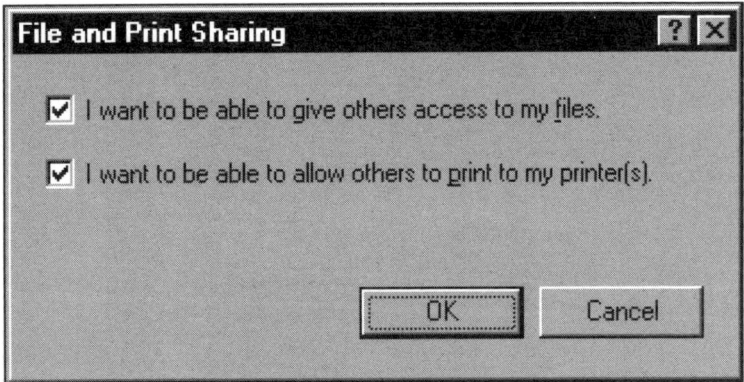

```
┌──────────────────────────────────────────────────┐
│ File and Print Sharing                     [?][X] │
│                                                    │
│   [✓]  I want to be able to give others access to my files. │
│                                                    │
│   [✓]  I want to be able to allow others to print to my printer(s). │
│                                                    │
│                  ┌──────────┐   ┌──────────┐      │
│                  │    OK    │   │  Cancel  │      │
│                  └──────────┘   └──────────┘      │
└──────────────────────────────────────────────────┘
```

Enabling Sharing

Ticking the above boxes does not allow specific folders and printers to be shared. This must be set in the My Computer or the Windows Explorer on *both machines*. Right click over the device or folder and select **Sharing....**

Now click the radio button to switch on **Shared As:** and if you prefer, change

the **Share Name:** which has been provided automatically.

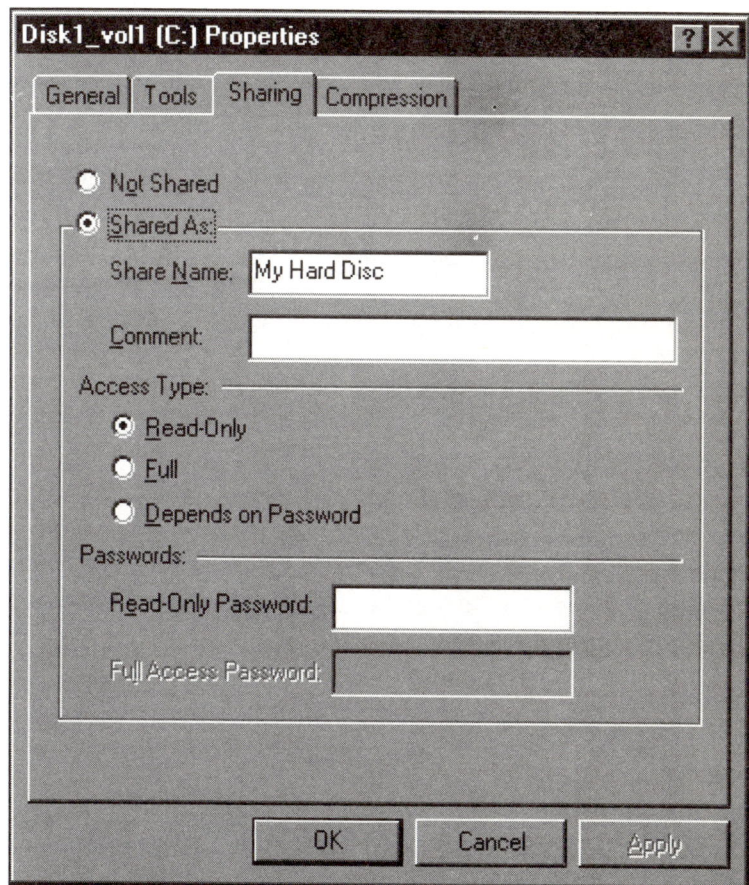

At this stage you can set the access to **Read-Only** or **Full** and set passwords for each type of access. After you click **Apply** and **OK** a small hand appears under the device or folder to indicate that sharing has been enabled.

To make a printer shareable a similar procedure is used to that for sharing disc drives and folders but you must first select the printer to be shared by locating it in the **Printers** folder (**Start**, **Settings**, **Printers**), while working on the machine to which the printer is attached.

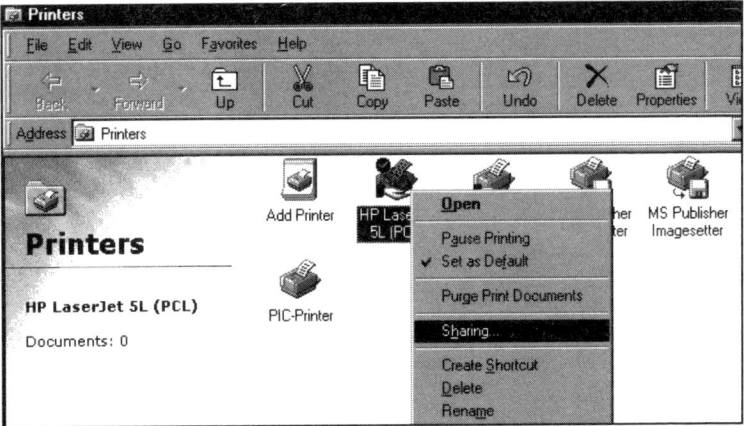

Then press the right button over the required printer and select **Sharing ...** . Switch on **Shared As:** and give the printer a new **Share Name:** and **Password:** if you wish.

Identification

Before you can connect the two computers on this simple network each machine must be identified uniquely with a **Computer name:** and **Workgroup:**. Each computer is set up using the **Identification** tab in the **Network** dialogue box accessed from **Start**, **Settings**, **Control Panel** and **Network**. The computer name can be up to 15 characters with no blank spaces. The workgroup should be the same for both computers.

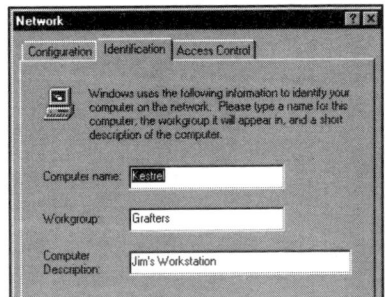

Making the Connection

We are now ready to make the connection having set up the network software components in Windows 98 and also set up sharing of the required resources such as disc drives, folders and printers. The basic arrangement is that one machine acts as the **Host** and the other is the **Guest**. The Host is the machine containing the shareable resources - disc drives, folders and printer(s). Either machine can act as the Host during a particular session provided the necessary resources have been set as shareable as previously described. Obviously the connecting cable must be in place and if you are using a parallel cable, you will need to fit a second parallel port if you are intending to share a printer. This is covered in **Appendix B: Fitting A Parallel Port Expansion Card**.

When you launch the **Direct Cable Connection** from **Start**, **Programs**, **Accessories** and **Direct Cable Connection**, a wizard allows you to set the machine as Host or Guest.

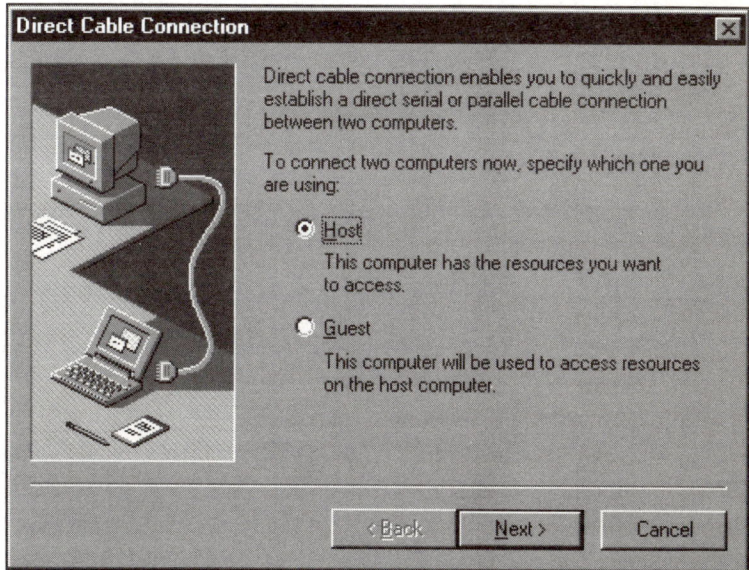

Then you have to select the port you wish to use.

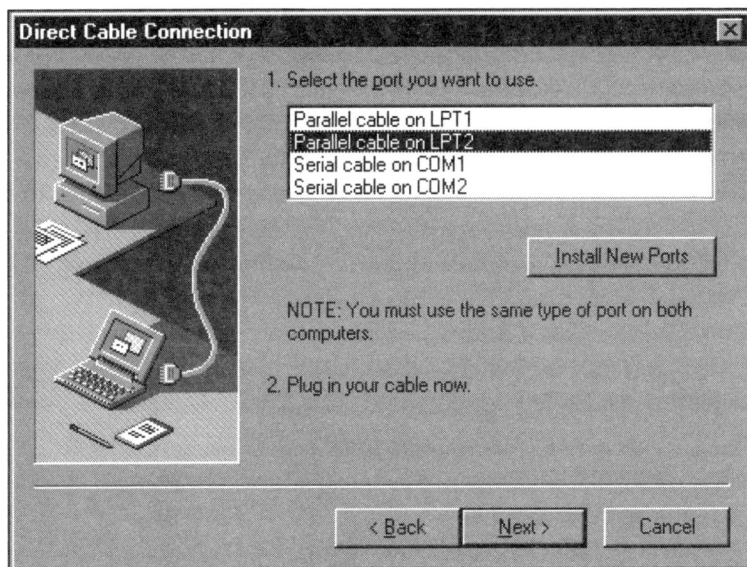

You must complete the wizard for both Host and Guest computers. Then the Host computer will **Listen** while the Guest makes a connection.

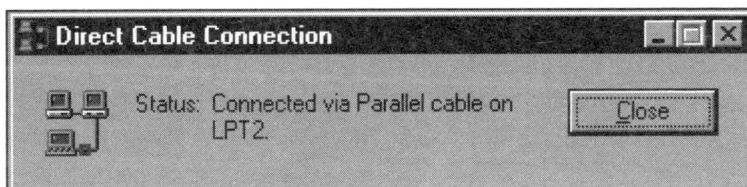

Once you are connected the Guest machine displays in a window on its screen a folder containing the shareable resources from the Host .

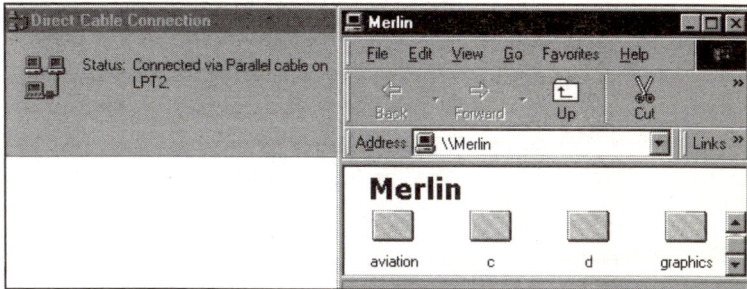

You can now open the Windows Explorer or My Computer and "drag and drop" folders or files from the Host machine to the Guest. Or you can use DCC to run Host-based programs on the Guest machine.

In future when you   start up the Direct Cable Connection, the connection is made by clicking a **Listen** button on the Host machine and a **Connect** button on the Guest machine.

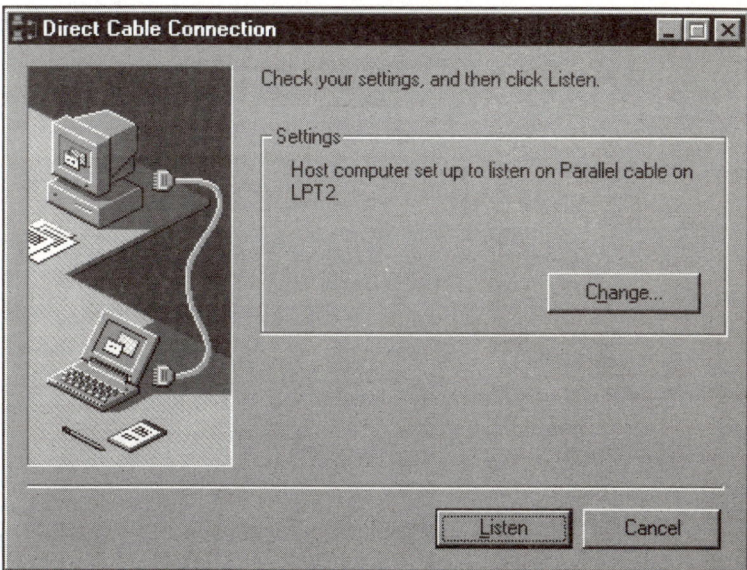

The **Change** button on each machine allows the Guest machine to become the Host and the previous Host to become the Guest.

Sharing a Printer

Apart form sharing discs and folders you can share resources such as printers over the **Direct Cable Connection**. The printer must be physically attached to the computer designated as Host. (You will need a second parallel port as described earlier). The printer must be set as shareable in the **Printers** folder of the Host machine (**Start**, **Settings**, **Printers**).

In my setup, the Host machine with the printer attached is identified as **Kestrel** while the Guest machine is **Merlin**. After you make the connection, the Guest **Merlin** displays a window showing the shareable resources of the Host **Kestrel**.

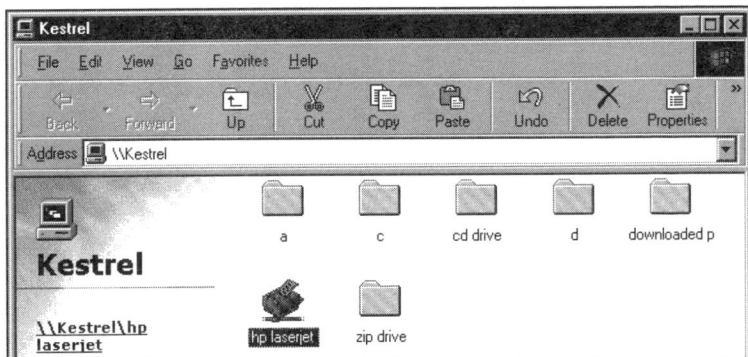

Included in the window on Merlin is the printer **Kestrel\hp laserjet**, which is attached to the Host machine. Double click the icon for the printer to start the process of setting it up as a shared "network" printer.

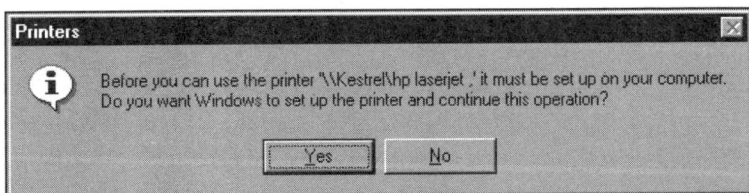

Clicking **Yes** starts the **Add Printer** wizard which mainly requires you to click **Next**. You will be asked to select the model of printer and to provide the printer driver files either from your Windows 98 CD or from a disc supplied by the manufacturer your printer. You are given the opportunity to change the name of the printer (as it appears on the Guest machine) and print a test page before clicking **Finish**. You should now be able to use the printer on both machines by selecting it in **Print** in applications such as Word or Paint.

The **Print** dialogue box displayed on the Guest machine Merlin is shown below. The full path of the network printer attached to **Kestrel,** the host machine, is given i.e. **\\Kestrel\hp laserjet**.

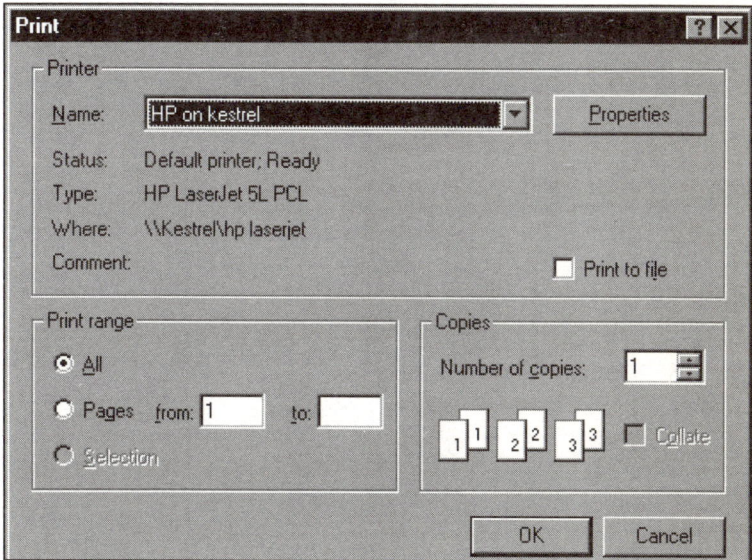

As mentioned previously, the Direct Cable Connection is an economical method of linking two computers, since all you need is a cheap cable - Windows 98 does the rest. However, better performance at greater cost can be obtained by connecting from 2-10 machines in a peer-to-peer network as discussed elsewhere in this book.

Summary: Simple Cable Connections

- A rudimentary network of two computers can be made economically by connecting their serial, parallel or USB ports with a short cable. This link can be used for sharing disc drives, folders and printers.

- Windows 98 contains all of the software needed to manage this system - known as the Direct Cable Connection. DCC and several essential software components must be installed from the Windows 98 CD.

- In the Direct Cable Connection, one machine is designated as the Host and the other as the Guest. The Guest displays in a window on its screen the *shareable* resources from the Host computer, permitting operations such as file transfer and printer sharing.

- Disc drives, folders and printers must be set as *shareable* in My Computer, the Windows Explorer or the Printers folder.

- A special cable is required for data transfer operations - a normal printer cable will not work.

- If using a parallel cable, the fitting of an extra parallel port is desirable.

- Data transfer over a cable linking the parallel ports is several times faster than using a cable connecting the serial ports.

- Third party software such as LapLink Professional from Traveling Software offers enhanced features for file transfer and remote computing. This includes support for a connection using a cable between the USB (Universal Serial Bus) ports. This is much faster than both the parallel and serial connections.

- Related topics such as LapLink Professional, the Universal Serial Bus and the fitting of extra parallel ports are covered in the appendices and elsewhere in this book.

- The Direct Cable Connection can perform a useful function if cost is a major consideration. Otherwise the building of a peer-to-peer network (described in later chapters) should be considered for connecting from 2-10 machines.

Introducing
Networks

Why Network?

Networks have been used for a long time in large businesses, colleges and other organisations because of the need to share files, applications software and printers. Also to provide a centralised backup facility and for internal communication and e-mail. Nowadays the demand for small networks in the home and small business is increasing. Many homes now have two or more computers and there's a need to share expensive devices like printers and scanners. Similarly why have a separate telephone line for each computer to connect to the Internet? Software is now available to enable several networked computers to share a single Internet connection.

Apart from sharing files, CDs and applications software including networked games you can also communicate with people in different parts of your house or business premises. Installing a network is relatively simple - it's basically a case of installing network interface cards in the computers then plugging the cables and connectors together.

Types of Network

There are two basic network configurations - **client/server** and **peer-to-peer**. The peer-to-peer network is perfectly suitable for the home and small office user, for whom this book is intended. However, expanding organisations may consider upgrading from peer-to-peer to the client/server model and so a comparison of the two types of network is given on the pages which follow.

The Client/Server Network

The client/server model is used for larger networks - typically from about ten machines up to several hundred. These may be contained within a single room or scattered through several buildings on a business site or college campus.

At the centre of the network is the server, often referred to as the *file server*. (You can also have *mail servers* and *print servers*.) The server is normally a more powerful computer than the users' workstations or *client* machines distributed around the network. The server and the clients must be fitted with network interface cards (NICs) and these provide the connections for the network cabling which links the computers. Networking hardware is discussed in detail in the next chapter.

The server normally has a more powerful processor, bigger memory and larger hard disc(s) to enable it to carry out its demanding role servicing the requests from the client machines. This will include running most of the applications software which is used around the network and dealing with printing. It will also act as the depository for the entire output of data files, wordprocessing documents, spreadsheets and other files produced by users of the client machines.

Although some software may be stored on individual client machines it is normal to buy a special network version of, say, a word processing or accounts program. This is installed on the server and run across the network by users of the client machines. Licences must be purchased to run multi-user software on a fixed number of computers. In education or training a single CD may be licensed and made accessible to all of the machines on the network. This can be achieved using either a shared CD drive or by copying the entire CD onto a special dedicated hard disc which acts as a CD server.

The server computer may also act as a *print server* to manage shared printing across the network although nowadays this role is often performed by a dedicated print server - a separate small hardware device which is plugged into the network in a suitable location.

It's normal for the server machine to be left running continually, including weekends and holidays. This enables users to go online at any time, perhaps from another building on the site. When the server is eventually shut down, this must be done according to a certain procedure. If the server were to suffer a sudden power failure, the resulting unsupervised shut down may damage the server and its contents. Servers on essential networks are fitted with an Uninterruptable Power Supply (UPS). This keeps the server powered up long enough for a shut down to be carried out according to the correct procedure.

As the server may contain all of the data files for an entire business or other organisation security may be vitally important. Should the server go down, the whole network will be out of action. All data files are backed up onto magnetic tape every day, with several tapes used in rotation and stored separately.

The client/server model is very efficient for the larger organisation, with its centralised resources. However, the client/server model is expensive and a large network requires highly trained IT professionals as network administrators. It really is too complex for enthusiastic amateurs to dabble in. The administrators' work includes the management of users and their login names and passwords, the installation of software and the scheduling of backups. Also the setting of access rights to files and directories, the removal of obsolete files, and protection against virus infection. Apart from troubleshooting any hardware problems there is also the issue of staff training in large organisations and possibly the design and maintenance of a company Web site or intranet. Even a small client/server network will require at least one well-trained member of staff and outside professional support for trouble-shooting and for making alterations.

The client/server model requires a dedicated network operating system such as Windows NT Server, Windows 2000 Server or Novell Netware and this can cost hundreds of pounds. These provide sophisticated facilities for organising users with login names and passwords and for managing files and tasks such as scheduled backups.

The cost of the server machine itself must also be considered, since in most cases it will be dedicated to its role as a file server and will not be available for use as a workstation.

The client/server network is a sophisticated and powerful system giving high performance and security. However, it's expensive to manage and maintain and therefore out of the reach of many home and small business users. The next section describes the peer-to-peer network which, although less sophisticated, is very successfully used in many homes and small organisations.

The Peer-to-Peer Network

The peer-to-peer network is eminently suitable for connecting a few machines (up to about 10) in the home, in a small office or perhaps a primary school. The peer-to-peer network uses the same basic networking hardware as the client/server model, i.e. cables connecting network interface cards in every machine. However, in the peer-to-peer network there is no dedicated server - all the machines have equal status. Also, there is no need for a special network operating system-everything you need is included within Windows 98.

Once the peer-to-peer network is set up, all of the machines and their shared resources can be viewed in the **Network Neighborhood**. This is part of Windows 98.

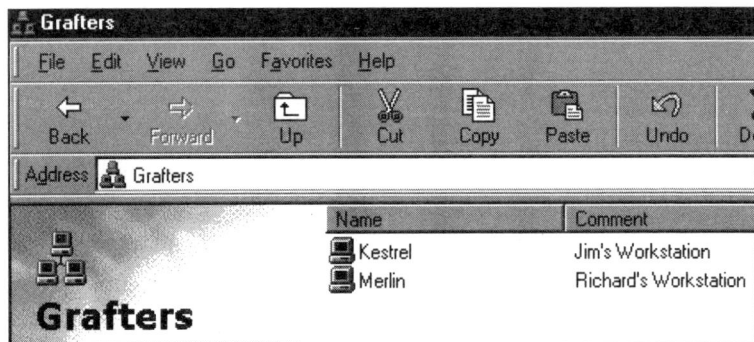

In the previous example there are two machines, Kestrel and Merlin in a peer-to-peer network. They are both members of the same workgroup, Grafters. Double clicking on the icon for either machine opens up a window showing its shareable resources - discs, folders, CDs, printers, etc. Folders and files may be copied between machines by dragging and dropping. This is discussed in detail in later chapters.

The peer-to-peer network provides much faster operations such as file transfer than the minimal network formed by linking the parallel or serial ports with a cable discussed in the previous chapter. Networking kits designed for the home or small business are becoming available very cheaply. The simplest consists of two network cards and the necessary cabling and connectors for under £20. Using the networking software components within Windows 98, this provides a very fast and efficient way of connecting two machines. While it lacks the sophisticated management, security and backup facilities of the client/server network, the peer-to-peer network has several advantages. For a small number of computers, it is easier to set up and manage and doesn't require specialist computer staff. It is also cheaper since there is no need to dedicate a machine as a server. One disadvantage is that if one computer is used for printing, the person working at this machine may notice a loss of speed if several people are trying to print at the same time.

Ethernet

Ethernet is a networking standard (used by both client/server and peer-to-peer networks) developed by the Xerox company in 1976. The Ethernet system includes the network interface cards, the cabling which connects the computers and the network protocol or communication language. Data is transmitted around the network in *packets,* each packet also containing a unique address for both the sending and destination computers. Every packet is delivered to every station on the network. The network cards "listen" for packets containing their address. Only when the station's address matches the delivery address will the data be received by the computer.

The jargon surrounding cabling and connectors can be very confusing with several obscure names appearing to describe the same object. Fortunately, with the increasing popularity of small networks there are now networking kits available which provide everything you need to connect two or three computers in a peer-to-peer network.

Thin Ethernet

The cheapest of these kits (under £20) includes two network interface cards and a **Thin Ethernet** cable to connect them. Also known as **Thinnet**, **Coaxial**, **Coax** and **10Base2**, this cable has a single copper centre and **BNC** bayonet connectors at each end. Although professionals use crimping tools to make up their own cables, ready-made cables can be purchased from computer suppliers. The cables are connected via T-pieces to the network cards at the back of the computer. The Thin Ethernet network has the computers arranged along the cable in a line - a configuration known as the **Bus** topology.

This requires each end of the cable to be fitted with a special **terminator**. These should be included in a Thin Ethernet kit but otherwise they are available cheaply from computer stores.

Thin Ethernet represents fairly old technology and is limited to a data transfer rate of 10 Mega bits per second. (8 bits typically being used to represent an alphabetical or numeric character). However, 10 Mbps is probably fast enough for most home networks - it seems stunningly fast when copying files. The T-pieces, each involving 3 bayonet connections, can be unreliable. In a network of many computers, with the bus technology, any break in the continuity of the cable will cause the whole of the network to fail. This can result in hours of "down time" until the break is detected.

However, in a home environment, especially if cost is a factor, a cheap Thin Ethernet network consisting of two network cards, a Thin Ethernet Cable, two T-pieces and two terminators is all you need to start networking with two machines. The system will work perfectly well over the distances likely to be encountered in the home or small business.

UTP (Unshielded Twisted Pair)

Also known as **10BaseT, UTP** is a later design of cabling used in many modern networks and looks similar to telephone cabling. Plug-in connectors fit into ports in the network interface cards. These ports are known as **RJ-45**s. The core of the cable comprises two copper wires twisted together and this design gives higher performance. Standard UTP cable (**10BaseT**) operates at 10 Mbps while a higher specification cable (known as **100BaseT**) has the potential to operate at the **Fast Ethernet** speed of 100 Mbps. For operation at 100 Mbps, a UTP cable classified as **Category 5** is recommended whereas 10 Mbps systems can use **Category 3**.

If you are connecting only two machines you can manage with two network cards containing RJ-45 ports and a special UTP **cross-over** cable obtainable from computer stores.

However, a preferred solution (even for a network of only two computers) is to connect the machines radially around a central **Hub** containing several RJ-45 ports. The computers are connected by individual cables like spokes around a wheel, an arrangement known as the **Star** topology. A major advantage of this configuration is that you can disconnect an individual computer and cable without disabling the rest of the network. Complete kits can be purchased from networking giants like 3Com for under £100 and these include the network cards, cabling and a hub containing several RJ-45 ports. You simply plug the UTP cables into the hub in the way that telephone cables plug into a jack socket. In large organisations computers may be up to 100 metres from the hub and extra hubs or **repeaters** can be inserted to increase the length of an arm of the network.

I have been using the 3Com OfficeConnect networking kit designed for the home and small business. It was easy to set up and has provided fast and reliable service for nearly a year. The Office Connect hub has several LEDs which give diagnostic information such as the status of the ports and whether or not packets of data are being sent or received. If you wish to expand your network, more hubs can be connected at a later date.

Summary: Introducing Networks

- Networking enables increasing numbers of computers in the home and small office to share expensive resources such as data files, applications software, printers, and CDs. Also to carry out tasks such as file transfer and backups.

- Software is available which allows several networked computers to share an Internet connection using one modem and telephone line.

- The peer-to-peer network connects all machines as equals; they can access each others' applications and data files and share a printer.

- The peer-to-peer network is relatively easy to set up and manage for small networks of 2-10 machines. Windows 98 contains all of the software needed to set up a peer-to-peer network.

- Complete kits are available containing all of the hardware for a peer-to-peer network.

- The client/server configuration is used for larger networks. The server is a powerful machine dedicated to the management of the network and used as a central store for the applications software and data files. A special network operating system is required such as Windows 2000 Server or Novell Netware.

- The client/server network has sophisticated systems for security and file management, including backups. These require the skills of a trained network administrator.

- Ethernet is the dominant standard for network technology such as network interface cards and cabling. Thin Ethernet is an older and slower type of cabling which requires computers to be connected in a continuous line, known as the Bus topology.

- UTP is a newer Ethernet specification, with the potential for faster operation, in which computers are connected around a central hub in the Star topology. The hub has diagnostic facilities and allows individual cables and machines to be removed without disabling the rest of the network, unlike the Bus configuration.

Installing the Hardware

The Network Interface Card

This is a small printed circuit board which connects each PC to the network cabling and enables communication with the other computers on the network. Also known as a *NIC* and a *network adapter*, the term *network card* will generally be used throughout this book. The network card is fitted to a spare expansion slot on your computer's motherboard (the main circuit board to which the principal components are connected).

Fitting the network card is a task which anyone can undertake, without special skills. It's just a case of removing the cover of your machine and plugging the card into one of the free slots on the motherboard. Network cards are available with either Thin Ethernet (BNC) connectors or UTP (RJ-45) ports. "Combo" cards allow both types of cable to be connected. If possible network cards designed for the computer's PCI slots should be obtained as these are easier to configure.

Before starting work you should rid yourself of any static electricity, as this can damage sensitive electronic components like the network card. You can earth yourself by touching a metal object such as the metal frame of your computer or part of a central heating system. Alternatively you can wear one of the special earthing straps which can be bought cheaply from electrical component suppliers. A well-lit room is desirable: it's also useful to have a small torch handy to illuminate the hidden depths of your machine.

With the machine switched off, disconnect all of the cables from the back of the computer. The casing can then be removed, usually after taking out some small retaining screws. You should see several spare slots of various types on the motherboard as follows:

Long black slots:	ISA architecture
Long brown slots:	EISA architecture
Short white slots:	PCI architecture

The documentation accompanying your network cards should specify the type of slot required by your particular card. If you have several spare slots all of the correct type, the card can be inserted into any one of them - position is not important. Now remove the blanking plate adjacent to the chosen slot by taking out and keeping safe the single retaining screw. Taking care not to touch the edges of the network card, firmly push it into the slot until the gold edge connectors are evenly engaged. Now secure the card by fitting the retaining screw. Replace the casing and reconnect the cables at the back of the machine.

PCMCIA Network Cards

Anyone using a notebook (or laptop) computer on the move will probably want to connect to a network on returning to base. Special credit card size Network Interface Cards are available which plug into a tiny slot on the computer. These cards are termed PCMCIA (Personal Computer Memory Card International Association), after the computer industry group which agreed on a specification for upgrade cards for portable computers. Two standards for peripherals (including network cards) are available, the earlier PC Card and the later, higher performance and more expensive CardBus.

PCMCIA cards are very easy to plug in and remove and installation of the necessary software drivers should be automatic. Like many components for notebook computers, however, PCMCIA cards are more expensive than the equivalent ISA or PCI components for full-size desktop machines. You need to insert network cards in every computer which is going to be networked, before starting to connect the cables.

Connecting the Cables

Before you can configure the network cards you need to install the cabling which links the machines together. If you are using coaxial cable (Thin Ethernet) then you must connect the cable to each machine using T-pieces or Y-pieces and fit terminators to each end of the cable.

If you're using twisted pair (UTP) cabling then each cable should be inserted into the RJ-45 port in a network card, before inserting the other end in an RJ-45 port in the hub. When all of the cables have been connected, the power to the hub should be switched on. A constant green light (LED) against the number for each port on the hub indicates that the card and its associated cabling are correctly installed. There may also be a green light on the network card suggesting that all is well. If there is no green light at the appropriate port on the hub, check that the cables are properly connected and the network card is firmly and evenly located in the slot on the motherboard. Obvious though it seems, it may be necessary to check that the hub is actually powered up!

Configuring the Network Card

The latest Plug and Play technology should ensure that each new network card requires very little setting up before it is ready to start work. If you buy PCI cards then they should be self-configuring. Normally the card is detected automatically when the computer is restarted. Then you are asked to insert the Windows 98 CD so that the appropriate drivers may be copied to your hard disc. All being well the network card is now ready for use, although the network software components in Windows 98 still need to be set up on each machine.

However, you may encounter problems which prevent the seamless, automatic configuration of your network cards as described above. The following pages therefore discuss some of the alternative methods available for detecting, configuring and examining the new network cards.

If you have ISA cards or cards which are not compatible with Plug and Play, then a little more work will certainly be necessary. The process of configuring a network card sets various parameters so that the new device integrates smoothly without clashing with other devices already installed in the computer.

This includes allocating an *interrupt setting (IRQ)* to the network card. An interrupt setting is the number of a channel which the device uses to communicate with the central processor of the computer. This number must be unique to the device; Two devices (such as a modem and a network card, for example) cannot share the same interrupt number if they are to operate simultaneously. In the past this was frequently a problem during hardware installation, requiring manual adjustment to the interrupt settings. Plug and Play technology is intended to alleviate this problem.

Before fitting the network cards pro-vided in the 3Com OfficeConnect Kit, you need to carry out a preinstallation procedure on each machine. Using software provided on floppy disc, the available interrupts are identified and a suitable one is assigned to the network card.

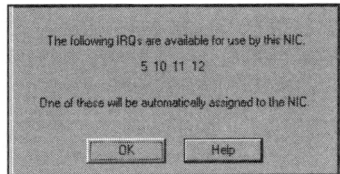

The following IRQs are available for use by this NIC.

5 10 11 12

One of these will be automatically assigned to the NIC

OK   Help

Before switching the computer on, you should make sure your Windows 98 CD and any discs provided by the manufacturer of your network card are available. These will probably be requested during the installation process.

After startup, the computer should announce that the network card has been detected as a new piece of hardware.

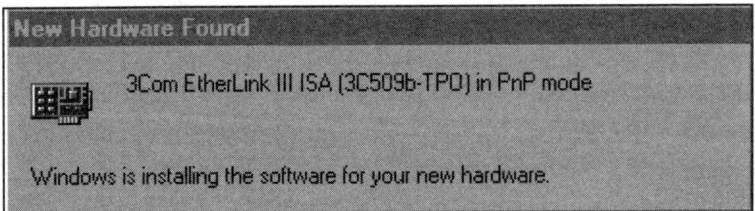

New Hardware Found

3Com EtherLink III ISA (3C509b-TPO) in PnP mode

Windows is installing the software for your new hardware.

If the network card is not detected automatically you can start the process by selecting **Start**, **Settings**, **Control Panel** and double-clicking on the icon **Add New Hardware**.

If the **Add New Hardware Wizard** fails to detect the NIC, you can do a manual installation by choosing to select your hardware from a list.

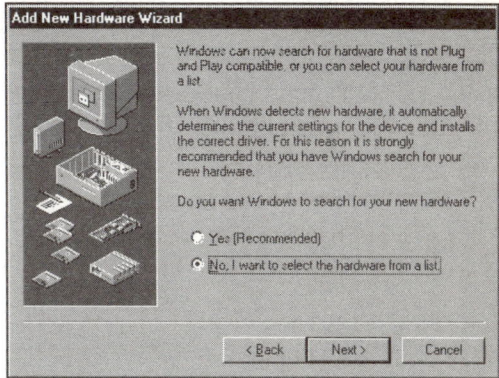

Then select **Network adapters** from the list of hardware types.

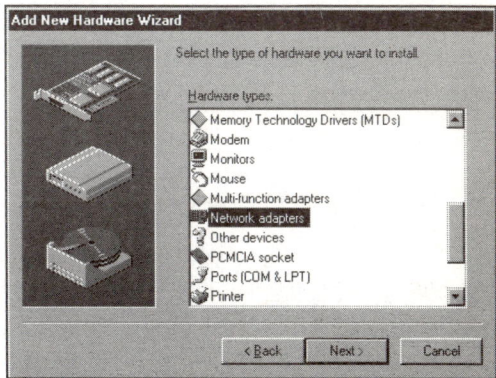

The **Select Device** window appears listing a range of manufacturers and models of network cards. You will need to select your particular card.

Select Device   ☒

Click the Network adapters that matches your hardware, and then click OK.
If you don't know which model you have, click OK. If you have an installation
disk for this device, click Have Disk.

Manufacturers: Models:

(detected net drivers)	3Com EtherLink III ISA (3C509/3C509b) in ISA mo
(Infrared COM port or dongl	3Com EtherLink III ISA (3C509b) in PnP mode
3Com	3Com EtherLink III ISA (3C509b-Combo) in PnP mc
Accton	3Com EtherLink III ISA (3C509b-TP) in PnP mode
Adaptec	3Com EtherLink III ISA (3C509b-TPC) in PnP mode

Have Disk...

OK   Cancel

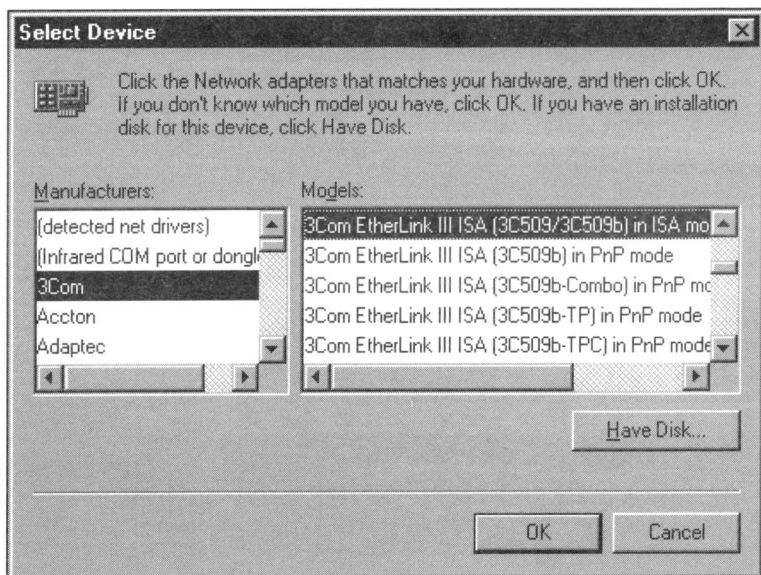

At this point you should click **Have Disk...** and you will be requested to
insert the floppy disc(s) provided by the manufacturer of your network
card.

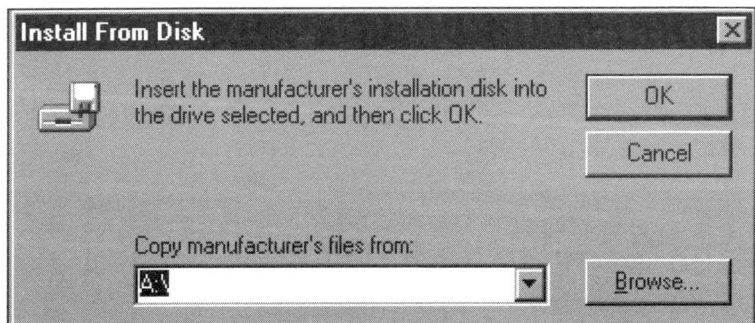

Install From Disk   ☒

Insert the manufacturer's installation disk into
the drive selected, and then click OK.

OK

Cancel

Copy manufacturer's files from:

A:\   ▼   Browse...

In general, the remainder of the configuration   procedure simply
involves following the instructions on screen while the network is
configured and the necessary files are copied to your hard disc.

In the 3Com OfficeConnect kit, an installation wizard automates the process and tests the card to ensure that it's working correctly.

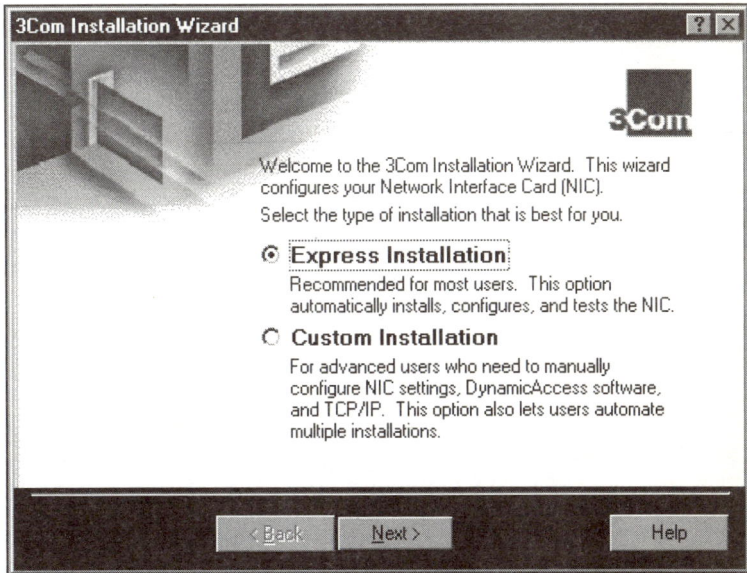

To complete the installation you will be prompted for the Windows 98 CD and after copying the necessary files you will be instructed to restart the machine.

Identifying Network Computers

At some point in the installation process you will be required to enter some names to identify each of the computers or "workstations" on the network. You make up the names yourself, with a limit of 15 characters and no spaces.

Computer name: is compulsory and must be *different* for each computer on the network.

Workgroup: is compulsory and must be the *same* for every computer in a group which are to share the same files or resources on the network

Computer Description: is optional.

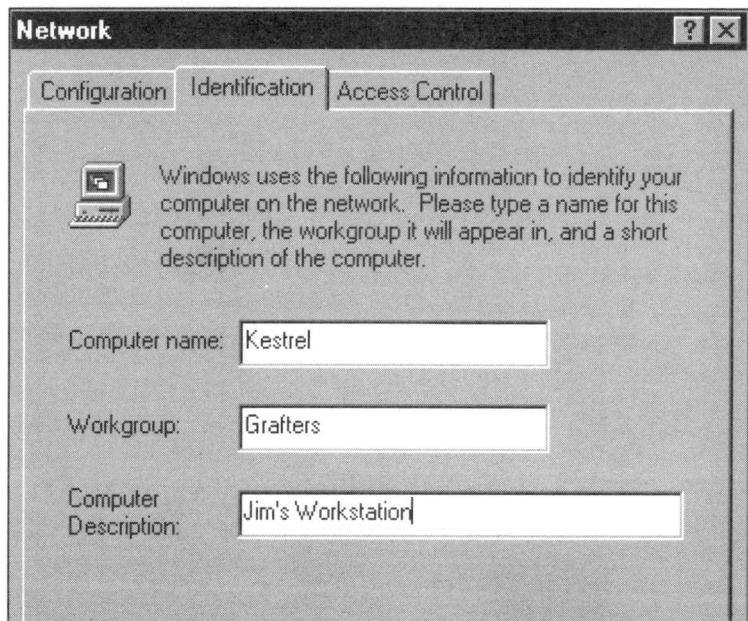

These names can be altered at any time by selecting **Start**, **Settings**, **Control Panel**, double-clicking the **Network** icon and selecting the **Identification** tab.

Examining the Network Card

You can check that your network card is working correctly using the **Device Manager** in the **Control Panel**. This is accessed by selecting **Start**, **Settings**, **Control Panel** then double-clicking the **System** icon before selecting the **Device Manager** tab.

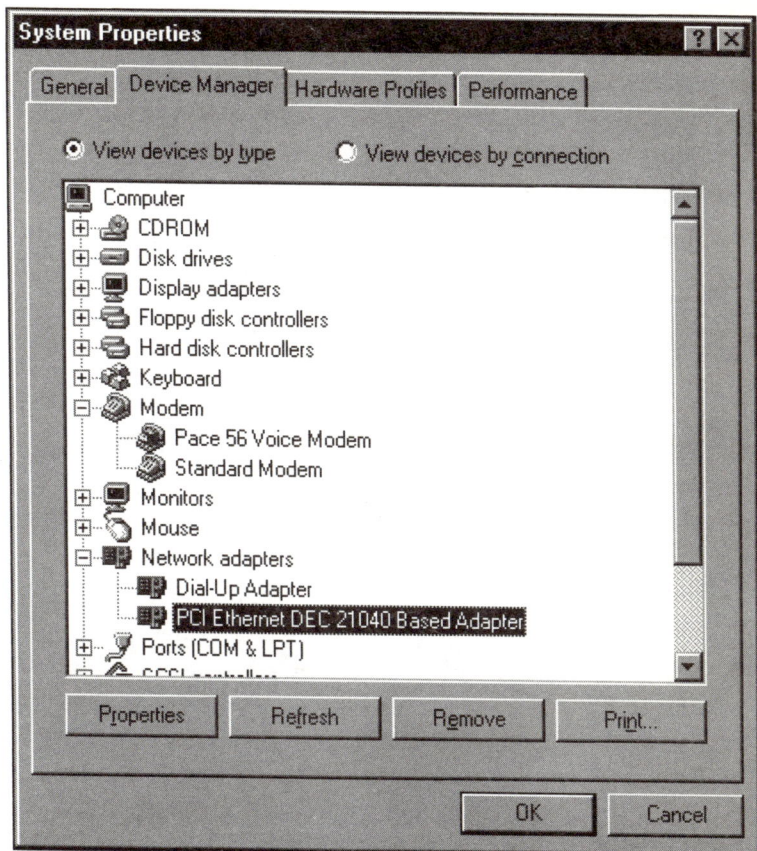

Selecting **Network adapters** should show the name of the network card which you have just installed. If there is any problem with the network card an exclamation mark in a yellow circle will appear through the icon for the device next to its name in the list.

With your network card highlighted in the device manager, clicking the **Properties** button should lead to the **General** tab and a message stating **This device is working properly**.

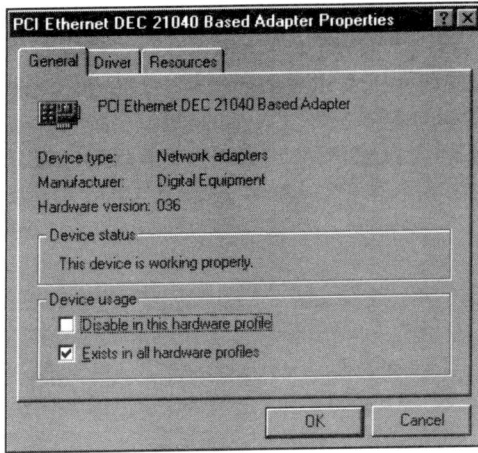

However, if an error is reported, selecting the **Driver** tab should provide help and the opportunity to re-install the network card driver software.

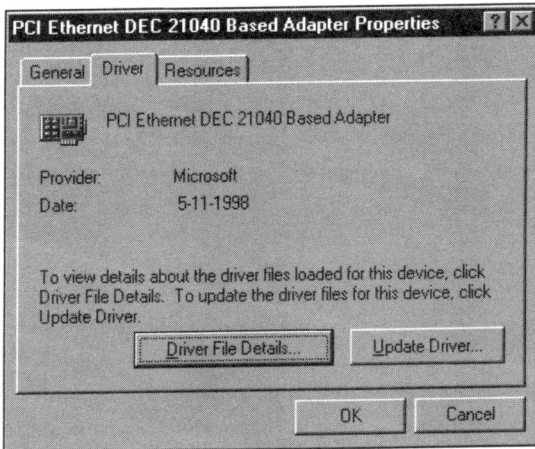

Buttons are provided to check the **Driver File Details...** or to **Update Driver...**.

If there is a problem with the IRQ (interrupt) setting on your network card, it may be possible to alter this after selecting the **Resources** tab for the network card.

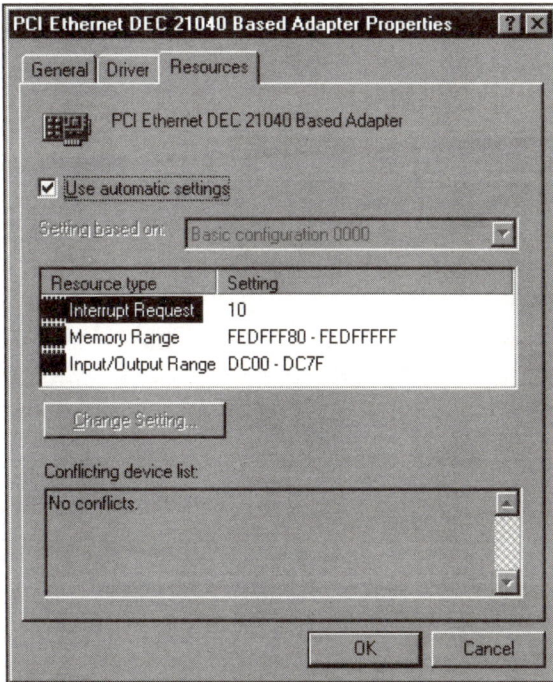

PCI Ethernet DEC 21040 Based Adapter Properties

General | Driver | Resources

PCI Ethernet DEC 21040 Based Adapter

☑ Use automatic settings

Setting based on: Basic configuration 0000

Resource type	Setting
Interrupt Request	10
Memory Range	FEDFFF80 - FEDFFFFF
Input/Output Range	DC00 - DC7F

Change Setting...

Conflicting device list:

No conflicts.

OK   Cancel

This should, all being well, display **No conflicts.** but if there are conflicts you can experiment with other settings by first switching off **Use automatic settings**. Now click **Change Setting...** and scroll through alternative values for **Interrupt Request**, **Memory Range** and **Input/Output Range** until **No conflicts.** appears in the **Conflicting device list:**.

The Windows 98 **Network Troubleshooter** accessed from **Start** and **Help** gives good diagnostic support for any remaining obstinate problems.

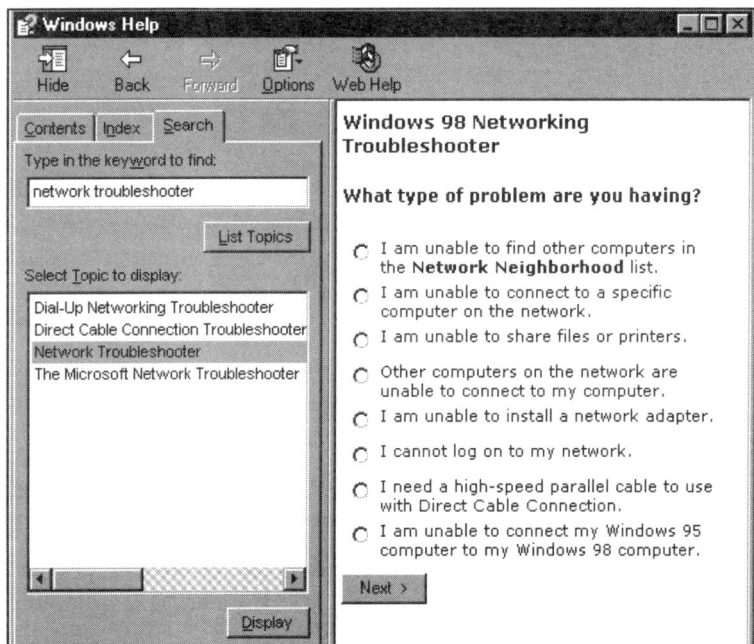

If you buy a 3Com network card, the **3COM NIC DOCTOR** diagnostic software is added to the Windows 98 **Start/Programs** menu as part of the installation process.

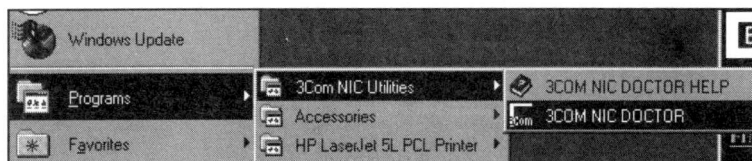

This includes utilities which test both the network interface card and the integrity of the network itself. Amongst other things it is also possible to alter the configuration of the 3Com card.

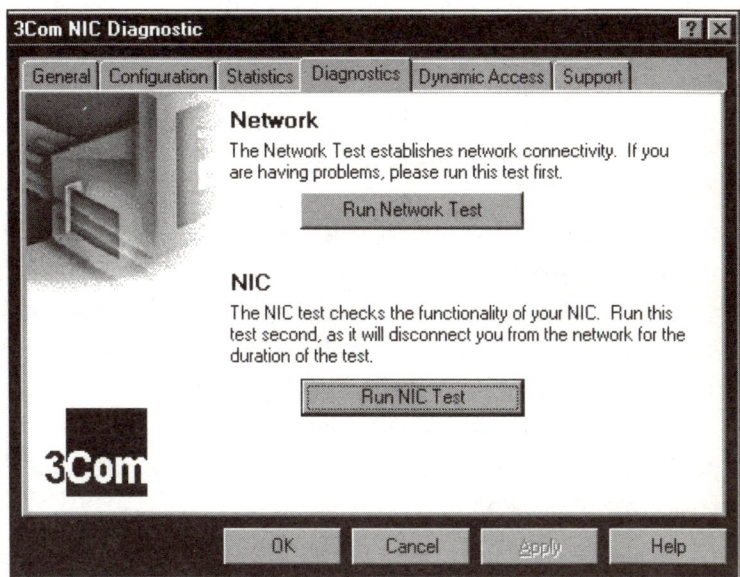

Before you can start to use the new network there is still some setting up to do in Windows 98. This involves making sure that the correct Windows 98 network software components are installed. Also ensuring that users of the network will be able to share folders and devices such as printers. These topics are covered in the next chapter.

Summary: Installing the Hardware

- Fitting network cards and connecting the cabling is a simple task which anyone can accomplish.

- The installation process involves the copying of driver software for your particular brand of network card. Also the setting of various parameters such as interrupts, to avoid conflicts with previously installed devices.

- PCI network cards are recommended as they are self-configuring and therefore very easy to install.

- The new network card should be detected automatically but if not, Windows 98 provides manual methods of detection and installation.

- To complete the installation you will need your Windows 98 CD and any discs provided by the manufacturer of the network card.

- All computers on the network must be individually identified with a unique *computer name*.

- All computers sharing the same drives, folders and resources must be members of the same *workgroup.*

- The status of the network card can be examined in the **Device Manager**, accessed by **Start**, **Settings**, **Control Panel** and **System** icon. This reports on any problems/conflicts and allows alternative settings to be tried. A yellow circle containing an exclamation mark indicates a fault with a device.

- Windows 98 includes a **Network Troubleshooter** which diagnoses and suggests solutions for a wide range of network problems.

Windows 98 Networking Software

Introduction

The previous chapter described the installation of network cards and cabling to allow your computers to communicate with each other in a small network. This will enable activities such as:

- Sharing folders, disc drives and CDs
- Sharing resources such as printers and modems
- Communication of messages and e-mail

Larger networks (upwards of 30 machines, say, but possibly hundreds) operate on the client/server model discussed earlier. This requires additional software in the form of a Network Operating System (NOS) to manage a multitude of tasks including file transfer, printing, backing up, e-mail and network security. Typical Network Operating Systems are Novell NetWare and Microsoft Windows NT 4. At the time of writing it is Windows NT4 is being succeeded by Windows 2000 Server and Windows 2000 Professional on the client machines.

Windows 98 contains all of the software components to run a small peer-to-peer network (typically 2-10 machines), without the need for specialist network management expertise demanded by the client/server configuration. In Windows 98 it's just a case of checking that the necessary components have been installed from the Windows 98 CD and adding any that are missing. The resulting network will lack some of the management and security features of a full client/server system but will nevertheless provide significant advantages over separate stand-alone machines.

The following work assumes that you have installed network cards in every computer and connected them using suitable coaxial or twisted pair cabling. Also that that they are working correctly; in the case of twisted pair cabling this is indicated by the presence of unflickering green lights on the cards and hubs. You should also have checked that the network cards are correctly configured and not conflicting with other devices. This is done by looking at **Network Adapters** in the **Device Manager/Properties/Resources** tab accessed from **Start/Settings /Control Panel** and double-clicking the **System** icon. Problems are reported by an exclamation mark in a yellow circle.

Setting Up Windows 98 Networking

(If you have previously set up a Direct Cable Connection as described earlier, you may already be familiar with some of the following topics.)

Before starting work, ensure that you have your Windows 98 CD conveniently to hand. To start the setup double-click the **Network** icon in the **Control Panel,** accessed from **Start** and **Settings**.

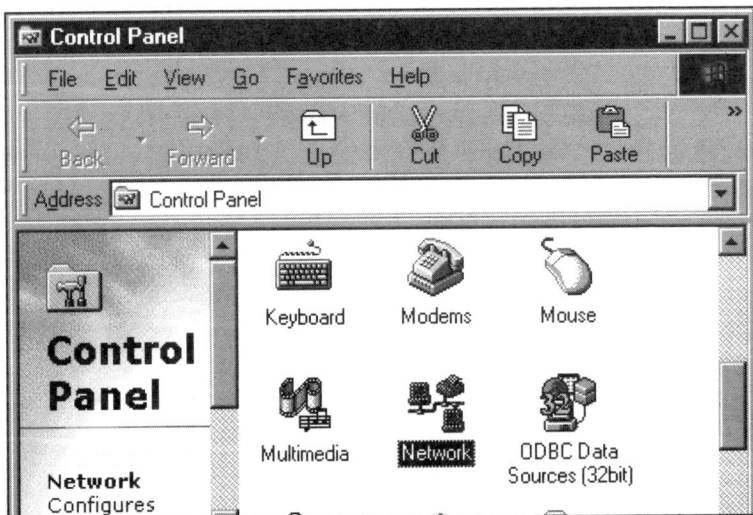

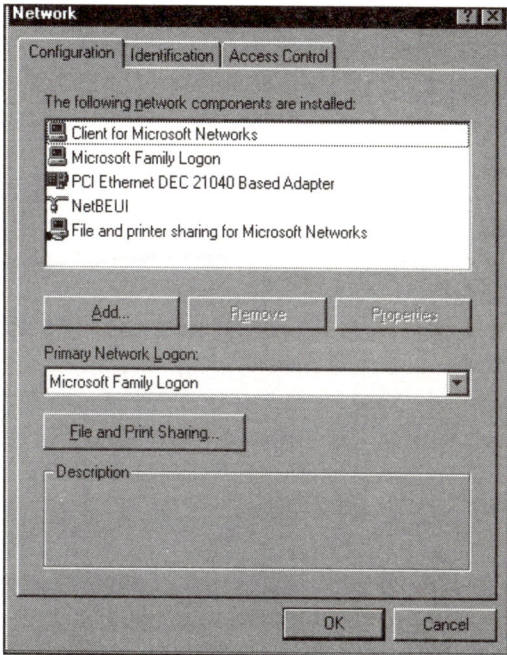

The **Network** window should open with the **Configuration** tab selected.

You need to check that certain components are present in the list. There may be other components included in your particular list, such as the **Dial-Up Adapter** and the **TCP/IP** protocol needed for Internet connection, but the following must be present *in every machine* for our small peer-to-peer network:

- **Client for Microsoft Networks**
- The name of your network card e.g. **PCI Ethernet DEC21040 Based Adapter**
- **NetBEUI**
- **File and printer sharing for Microsoft Networks**

These components are described on the next page, together with the method of installing them if they are not already present.

Client for Microsoft Networks

This is software which allows you to connect to other computers and to share files and resources such as printers.

To install this component, from the **Network Configuration** dialogue box select **Add...** then **Client**.

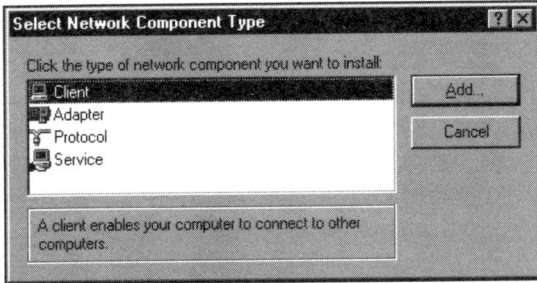

Now select **Add...** then **Microsoft** and **Client for Microsoft Networks**.

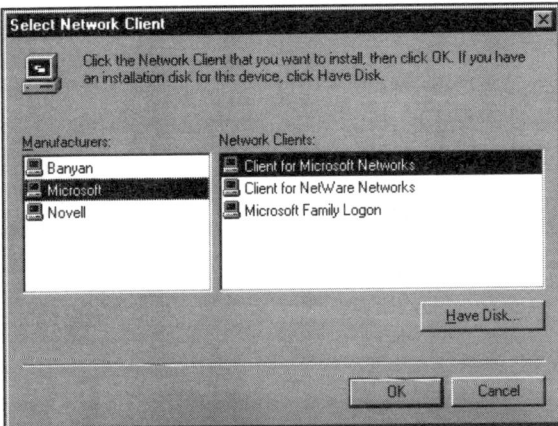

Click **OK** and you will be asked to insert the Windows 98 CD to install the component. **Microsoft Family Logon** can be added in the same way from the list of **Network Clients:** (if necessary). This is used when Windows starts, to display a list of users and allow a user to log on with their Windows 98 password. If you select **Client for Microsoft Networks** as the **Primary Network Logon:** in the **Network** dialogue box you will be asked to log on with the *network* user name and password.

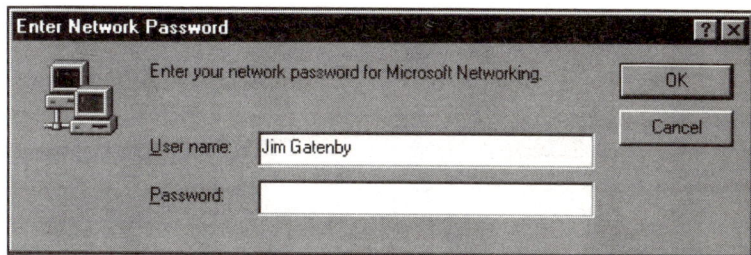

Adapter

If the name of your network card doesn't appear on the list of components in the **Network Configuration** dialogue box, then you need to check the installation of the network card as described in the previous chapter. If necessary, refer to the **Network Troubleshooter** in **Help**, accessed from the Windows 98 **Start** button. If you need to install your card again or to change it for any reason, select **Add...** in the **Network Configuration** dialogue box and then **Adapter**.

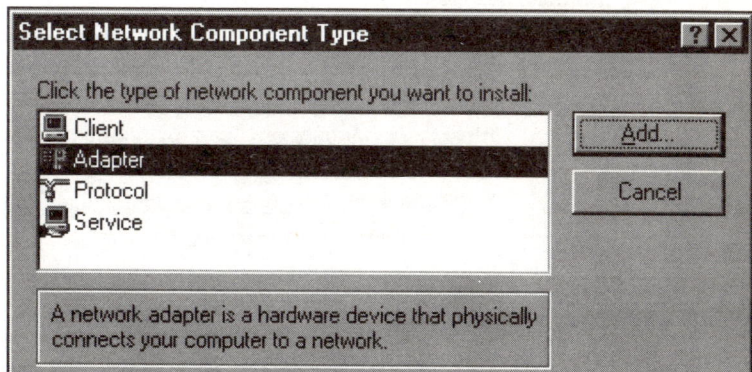

When you select **Add...** you are given the chance to select your network card from a list of manufacturers and models. You will need to have Windows 98 CD and any discs provided by the manufacturer of your network card.

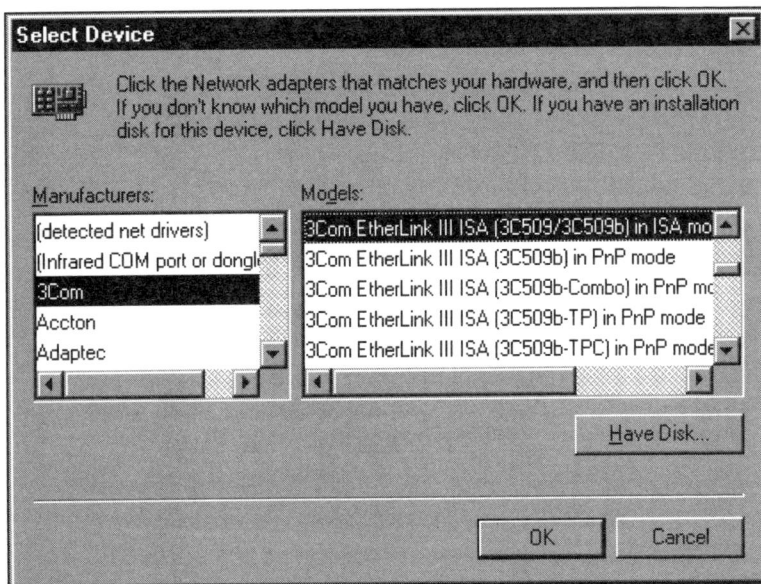

Please see the previous chapter for more information on installing a network card.

NetBEUI

This is one of the protocols or languages used by computers to communicate over a network. Other protocols include TCP/IP, used to connect computers on the Internet. NetBEUI is particularly suitable as a protocol for computers on small peer-to-peer networks.

To install NetBEUI, from the **Network Configuration** dialogue box select **Add...** then **Protocol**.

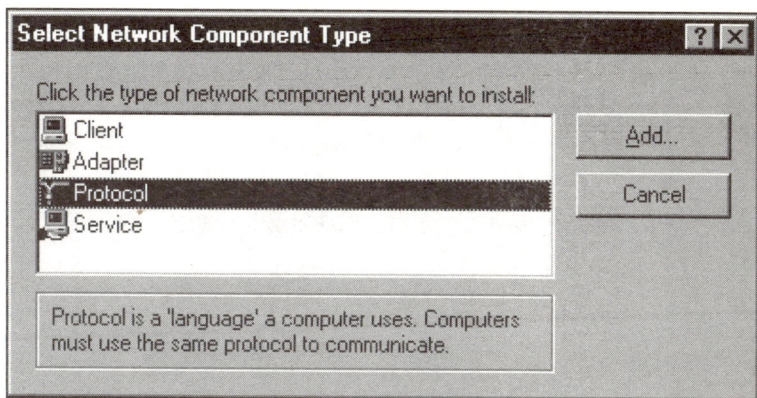

Now click **Add...** again and select **Microsoft** from the list of manufacturers which appears. Scroll down through the list of protocols until you can select **NetBEUI**, then click **OK**.

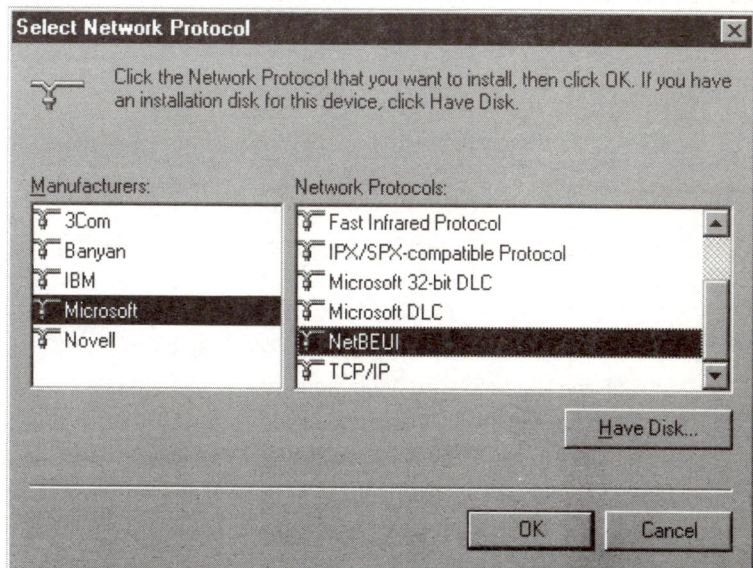

File and Printer Sharing

The last essential network configuration component, **File and printer sharing for Microsoft Networks** is designated as a **Service**. From the **Network Configuration** dialogue box click **Add...** then select **Service**.

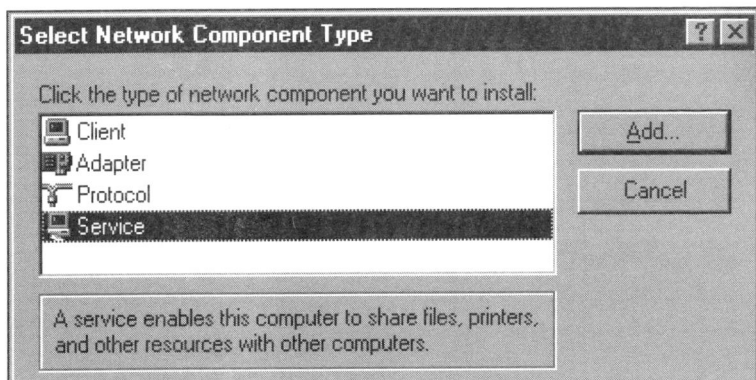

If you now select **Add...** again you are presented with a choice of Network Services.

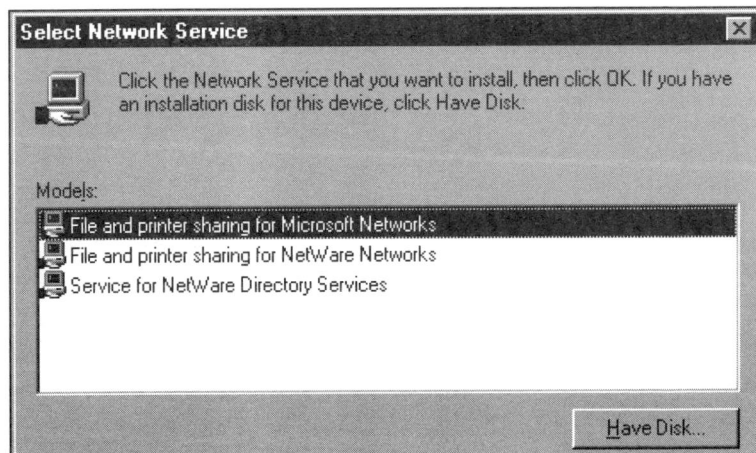

Select **File and printer sharing for Microsoft Networks** and click **OK**.

To allow other people to actually share files and printers, from the **Network Configuration** dialogue box, click the button **File** and **Print Sharing...**. Then make sure both options are ticked in the **File and Print Sharing** box.

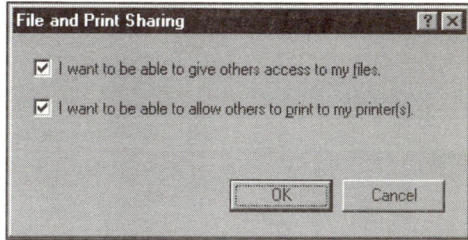

Although we have configured Windows 98 to permit the sharing of files and resources, we still need to designate the individual files and resources as "shareable". This is discussed shortly.

Identification

Before leaving the main **Network** configuration dialogue box check that the identity for each machine on the network has been correctly set. This was discussed in detail in the previous chapter, but as a reminder, each machine must have a unique name (up to 15 characters, with no spaces) and each machine must be a member of the same work group as every other machine with which it is to share files and resources. Click the **Identification** tab in the **Network** dialogue box to check the details.

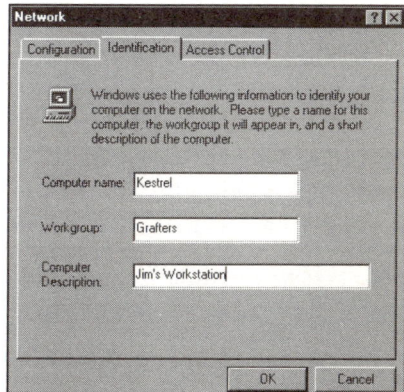

The final tab on the **Network** dialogue box is **Access Control**. Selecting this allows you to specify how access is controlled to the shared files and resources such as printers and CD drives. Each resource may be protected by a password or alternatively access may be restricted to specified users or groups. For a small peer-to-peer network we need to make sure the radio button for **Share-level access control** is switched on.

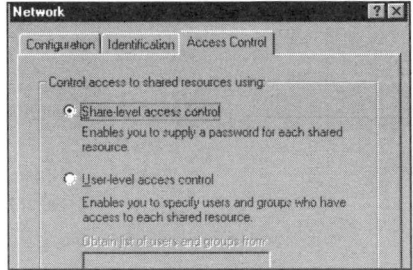

Sharing Resources

We have almost completed the setup of our small peer-to-peer network. We have enabled **File and printer sharing for Microsoft Networks** but we have not yet designated any individual resources as *shareable*. During this process the level of access to folders, drives and printers is set at either **Full** (both read and write operations are possible) or **Read Only**. (If a folder is designated as **Read Only** you cannot alter any of the files within it.) The need for passwords to individual resources can also be specified.

Sharing can be initiated in **My Computer** after double-clicking its icon on the Windows 98 desktop. Suppose you want to make the whole of the **C:** drive shareable by all members of the workgroup. Right click the device you want to make shareable.

Then select **Sharing:** from the resulting menu. Individual folders can be designated as shareable after right-clicking them in **My Computer** or **Windows Explorer**. The **Properties** dialogue box should open with the **Sharing** tab selected.

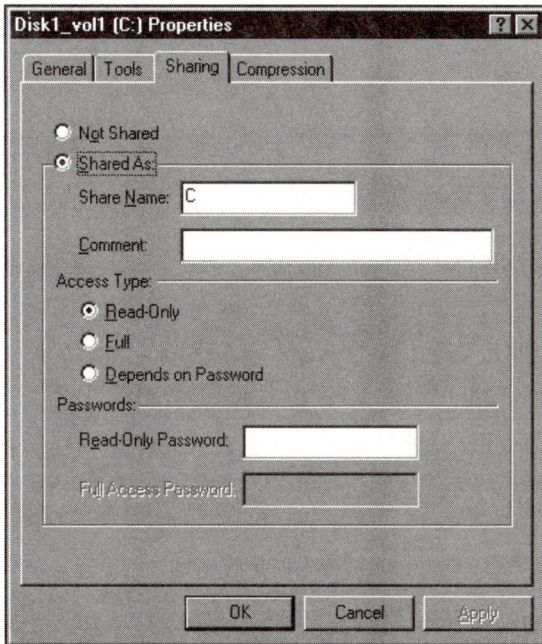

First switch on the **Shared As:** radio button. Then if you wish, a new **Share Name:** can be given to the resource or you can accept the name already provided by Windows 98. This is the name which other users will see on their computer screens when sharing resources. There is also a slot for you to enter an additional descriptive comment if you wish.

Security

On large networks, the issue of security can cause enormous problems for network managers. I know from personal experience of managing a large college network that beating the security system holds a magnetic attraction for curious young minds. However, the use of passwords to prevent unauthorised access can be a mixed blessing. If the chosen passwords are too obvious, like the name of your dog, for example, they are easily guessed. Conversely, if you make passwords deliberately obscure, people who make only occasional use of the network tend to forget them and files then become inaccessible. Additionally the most determined hackers may find out how to change the passwords, making resources unavailable to the ordinary user.

Despite these difficulties, every precaution must be taken to safeguard files which are valuable for commercial, personal or academic reasons. It goes without saying that important files should be backed up onto a separate storage medium such as disc or tape and stored in a separate, secure physical location.

Read-Only

If you switch this radio button on, users of other computers will be able to read and copy files, but not alter or delete them. If you wish to restrict **Read-Only** access to authorised users you can add an optional password.

Full

Switching on this radio button allows the user of other machines on the network to read files, modify or delete them.

Depends on Password

With this facility switched on, users will gain either **Read-Only** access or **Full Access**, depending on which of two passwords they enter.

After you have set up the access type and any passwords, click **Apply** and **OK**. Any resources which you have made shareable are denoted by a small supporting hand in **My Computer** (or **Windows Explorer**) .

In the example above, the floppy drive, hard drive (volumes 1 and 2), Zip and CD drives have all been designated as shareable.

Setting Up Shared Printing

Sharing a printer is one of the best reasons for networking. It wouldn't make economic sense to equip every computer with its own laser or inkjet printer when one device can easily service the whole of a small network. Or you may wish to give every machine on the network the choice of different types of printer. With a small peer-to-peer network (up to 10 machines, say), it should be possible to continue to use the computer (which has the printer attached) as a normal workstation.

So someone can carry on word processing, say, while their computer controls the network printing. On larger networks, the amount of traffic to the printer makes it necessary for a dedicated computer or special *print server* device to be assigned to the task of controlling the printer.

There are two stages to setting up network printing:

1 Make the network printer shareable.

2 Set up each workstation on the network to use the printer.

Making a Printer Shareable

Open the **Printers** folder in **My Computer** by selecting **Start, Settings** and **Control Panel** and double-clicking the **Printers** icon. Right-click the mouse over the name of the printer to be shared.

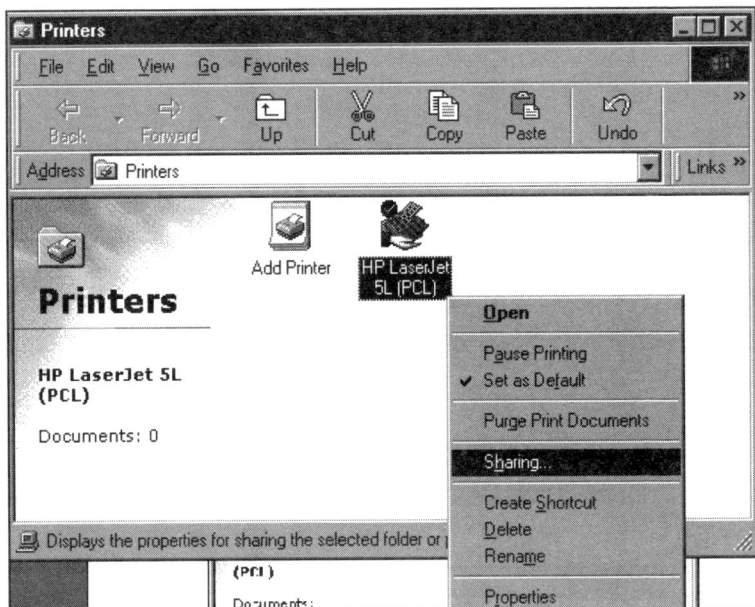

If you now select **Sharing...** from the drop-down menu, the printer **Properties** dialogue box should open at the **Sharing** tab.

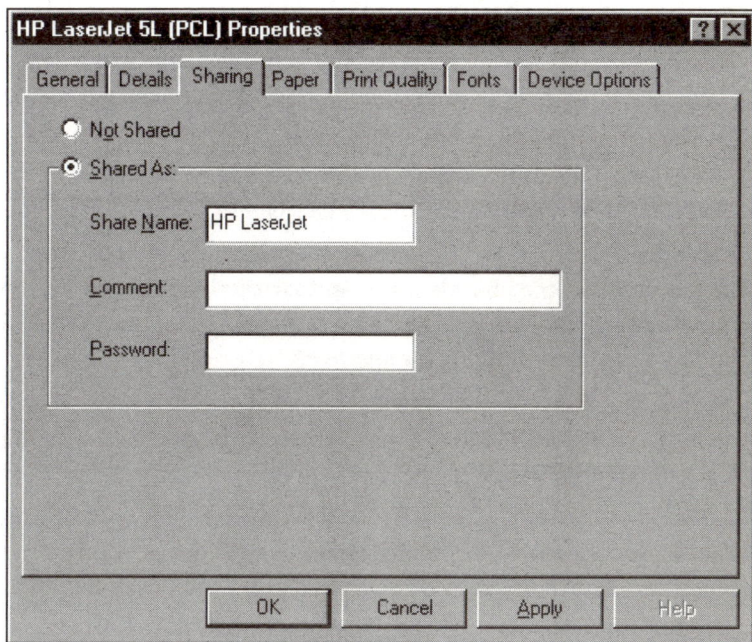

```
┌─────────────────────────────────────────────────────────────┐
│ HP LaserJet 5L (PCL) Properties                       [?][X] │
├─────────────────────────────────────────────────────────────┤
│ General │ Details │ Sharing │ Paper │ Print Quality │ Fonts │ Device Options │
│                                                              │
│    ○ Not Shared                                              │
│    ◉ Shared As:─────────────────────────────────────┐        │
│    │                                                 │        │
│    │  Share Name:  │HP LaserJet          │           │        │
│    │                                                 │        │
│    │  Comment:     │                     │           │        │
│    │                                                 │        │
│    │  Password:    │                     │           │        │
│    │                                                 │        │
│    └─────────────────────────────────────────────────┘        │
│                                                              │
│          ┌────────┐  ┌────────┐  ┌────────┐  ┌────────┐      │
│          │   OK   │  │ Cancel │  │ Apply  │  │  Help  │      │
│          └────────┘  └────────┘  └────────┘  └────────┘      │
└─────────────────────────────────────────────────────────────┘
```

Switch on the radio button for **Shared As:**. If you prefer, a different **Share Name:** from the one supplied by Windows 98 can be used to identify the printer on the network. You can also add a **Comment:** and a **Password:** at this stage. Now click **Apply** and **OK** and the printer should be available to be shared by the other workstations on the network, confirmed by a hand under the icon in the **Printers** folder.

However, before all computers on the network can actually use the remote printer, some setting up on the individual workstations is necessary. This is covered in the next chapter describing the use of the network in the **Network Neighborhood**.

Summary: Windows 98 Networking Software

- Windows 98 contains all of the software needed to set up and manage a peer-to-peer network (assuming network cards are already installed and correctly configured in every machine).

- The necessary software components are included on the Windows 98 CD and must be added to every computer on the network, if they are not already present.

- The four essential components are: **Client for Microsoft Networks**, the driver software for your network cards, a protocol such as **NetBEUI** and **File and Printer Sharing for Microsoft Networks**.

- Installing the software components is carried out using the **Add...** button in the **Network** dialogue box, accessed by double-clicking its icon in the **Control Panel**.

- All resources which are to be shared across the network such as folders, disc drives, CDs and printers, must be designated as *shareable*. This is done in **My Computer** or **Windows Explorer**, working at the computer where the resource is installed or attached.

- Security options include **Read Only** access to files or **Full** access, which allows files to be modified.

- *Passwords* may be added to resources so that only authorised users may gain access. Additionally the type of access (Read Only or Full) may depend on which password the user enters.

The Network
Neighborhood

Introduction

At this stage we have installed the hardware on each computer on the network and set up each machine with the Windows 98 network software components. When you start each machine on the network, the **Network Neighborhood** icon should appear on the Windows 98 desktop. Opening this reveals all of the computers connected to the network. The Network Neighborhood is the means by which you can "see" the shared resources of the other machines on the network. This enables you to carry out tasks such as copying files, sharing CD drives and printing across the network. The **Network Neighborhood** is opened by double-clicking its icon on the Windows 98 Desktop.

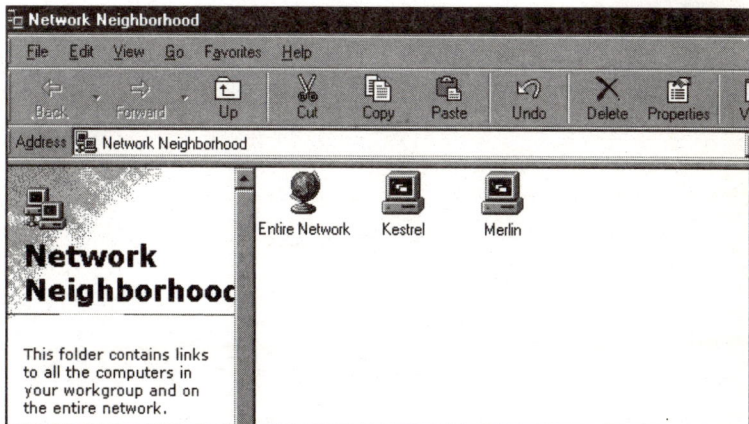

In the previous screenshot you can se that my small network consists of two computers, **Merlin** and **Kestrel**. You can display more information by selecting **View** and **Details** from the **Network Neighborhood** menu bar.

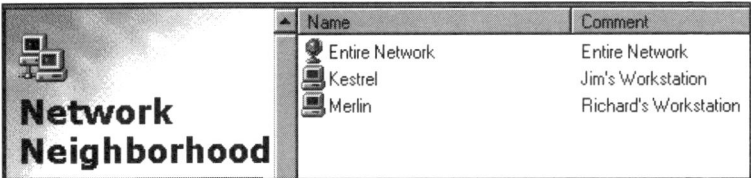

Double clicking on the icon for a computer on the network reveals the shared resources available on that computer. Note that in order for resources (drives, folders and printers, etc.) to appear in the **Neighborhood Network**, they must have been designated as *shareable* in **My Computer** or the **Windows Explorer**.

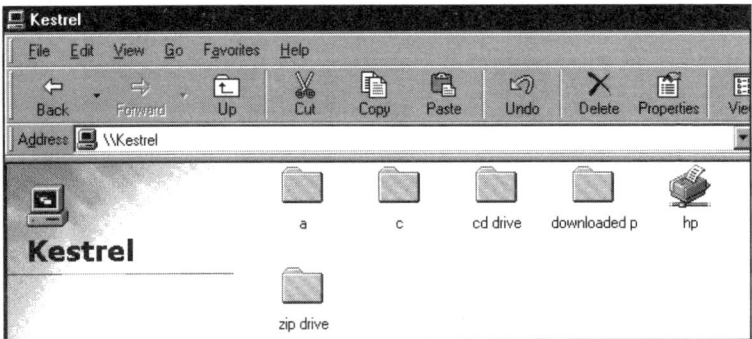

You can see that my machines can share drives **a:** and **c:** on the **Kestrel** computer, as well as the **zip drive** and **hp** printer. The **cd drive** is also available to all machines on the network. No matter which machine we work at, the same view of all machines appears in the Network Neighborhood. Each machine has equality with any other - hence the title peer-to-peer network.

You can display the shareable resources of two (or more) machines, simultaneously on the screen. Open up the first machine by double-clicking on its name in the **Network Neighborhood**. Then open up the second machine in the Network Neighborhood. Now right-click the mouse on an empty part of the **Taskbar** at the bottom of the Windows 98 screen. Select **Tile Windows Vertically** and the shareable resources of the two (or more) computers should appear side by side on the screen.

Now you can use the **Network Neighborhood** to copy folders and individual files just as you would in **My Computer** or the **Windows Explorer**. Simply open up the appropriate drive then drag and drop the required item onto the window for the other machine.

Once set up, the peer-to-peer network is a very fast and easy method of transferring files between machines. It is infinitely more efficient than physically swapping floppy discs between machines. You can easily copy files from the CD drive on one machine to the hard disc of another computer which doesn't have a CD fitted. As an example I copied a folder of 30Mb in size from the CD drive of one machine to another computer's hard disc. The task was very simple and took about a minute. Transfers of similar magnitude would be very laborious using floppy discs, even with file compression.

Drive Mappings

As users of standalone computers we soon become familiar with the idea of letters to represent resources. **C**: is normally used for the hard disc, **A**: for the floppy disc and **D**: or **E**: for the CD ROM drive. On a network linking many machines this form of identification is inadequate since each machine will have a **C**: drive. To identify a specific **C**: drive, for example, you would need also to include the name of the particular workstation. Drive mappings overcome this problem by enabling a resource such as a hard disc, CD drive or ZIP drive to be given a letter which identifies it throughout the entire network. (A drive mapping can also be used to point to a specific *folder* which has been made shareable rather than an entire disc drive or CD drive).

So, for example, the **C**: drive on my Kestrel computer could be mapped as **H**: and this would be its identification on the other computers throughout the network. Drive **H**: would be available to every workstation and be used just like their local floppy and hard drives. Similarly a remote ZIP drive on one workstation could be mapped as **J**: for example and used by every other workstation for backing up files. (The computer with the shared resource attached continues to use the original local drive letter to access the resource).

As a practical application of drive mappings, a machine without a CD drive attached could use a mapping, **K**:, say to a CD drive on a remote machine. Using drive **K**: in the same way as any other drive **A**:, **C**: or **D**: etc., you can access the remote CD drive. This would enable you, for example, to install CD-based software onto the hard disc of a machine which doesn't have a CD drive fitted.

You create drive mappings to a resource while working on a machine which is remote from the resource. For example, I might want to set up a mapping to the ZIP drive which is attached to the Kestrel computer, so that other machines on the network can use it.

First, while working at the Merlin computer, the window for the Kestrel computer is opened up in the **Network Neighborhood;** this reveals only those resources which have been designated as shareable.

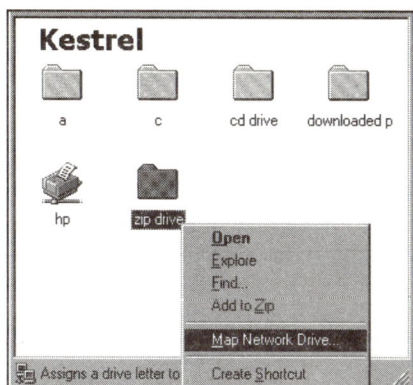

Then right click on the icon for the ZIP drive. A drop down menu appears from which you can select **Map Network Drive…**. The next menu allows you to choose a mapping from a list of available letters.

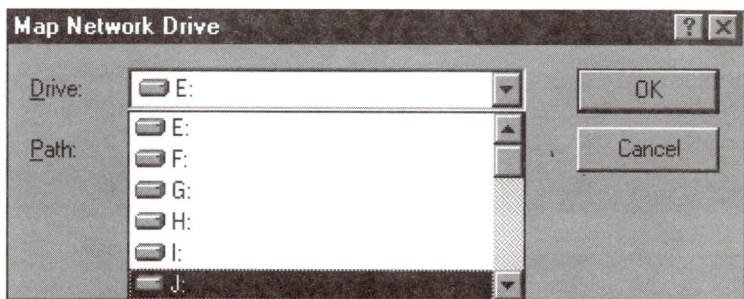

Switch on **Reconnect at Logon** to make this a permanent mapping then click **OK**.

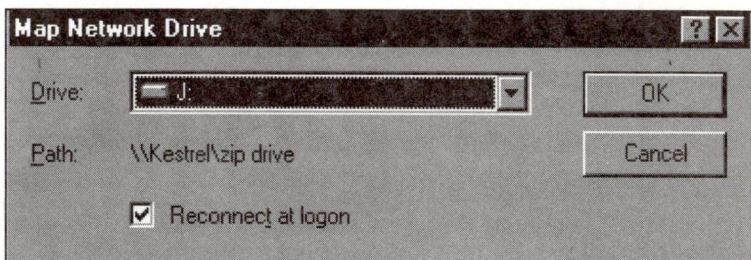

Every computer on the network (other than the one with the ZIP drive attached) should now see the ZIP drive as drive **J:**. It can be accessed to save and retrieve files through the **File** menus and to make backup copies. Although it is a remote resource, the drive mapping enables it to be used with the convenience of a local drive.

The following screenshot shows **My Computer** for the Merlin machine.

Drives **A:**, **C:** and **D:** are the local drives physically built into the computer. Drive **J:** is the ZIP drive fitted to another machine on the network (the **Kestrel**). Drive **J:** can be accessed for **File**, **Open** and **Save** operations by any machine on the network other than the machine to which the ZIP drive is attached. (Provided the resource has been set to   **Full** in the **Access Type:** as discussed in the previous chapter). Access will also depend on the use of any passwords which have been set.

Mapping with Windows Explorer

You can also create and remove drive mappings in Windows Explorer.

Open the **Windows Explorer** by right-clicking the **Start** button and selecting **Explore** from the menu. From the Windows Explorer menu bar select **Tools** and **Map Network Drive...**.

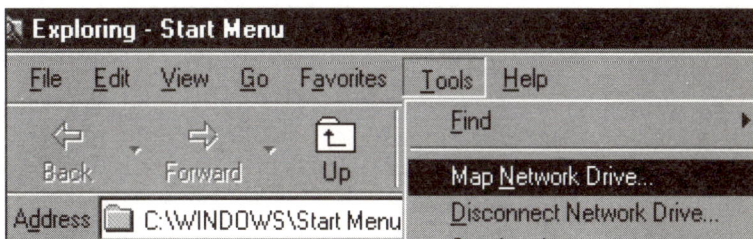

The **Map Network Drive** dialogue box appears allowing you to select a letter (**K:** in this example) for the new mapping.

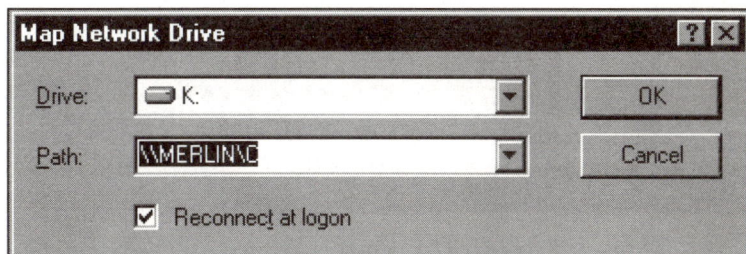

In **Path:** select from the drop down menu the resource you wish to map as a network drive. Here I selected **\\MERLIN\C** the path to the shareable hard disc **C:** drive on machine Merlin. On completion of the mapping process, any of the workstations can access this drive simply by selecting drive **K:**. To make this a permanent mapping every time you log on, click to place a tick next to **Reconnect at logon**. Omitting the tick will disconnect the mapping when the computer is switched off. Click **OK** to complete the mapping.

Removing a Drive Mapping

From the Windows Explorer **Tools** menu, select **Disconnect Network Drive....** Highlight the drive(s) you wish to remove and click **OK** to remove the mapping.

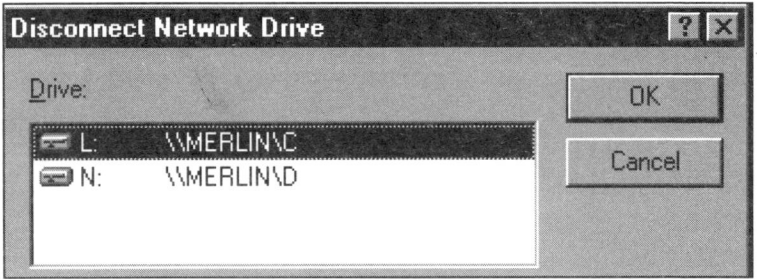

```
Disconnect Network Drive                    ? X

Drive:                              ┌──────────────┐
                                    │      OK      │
  L:      \\MERLIN\C                └──────────────┘
  N:      \\MERLIN\D                ┌──────────────┐
                                    │    Cancel    │
                                    └──────────────┘
```

Printing Across the Network

In this section we enable all machines to share a single network printer. The network must be set up and working so that each computer can "see" other machines on the network. The network printer must be attached to a computer and working correctly. It must have been designated as shareable in the **Printers** folder in **My Computer** as described in the previous chapter. You need to have your Windows 98 CD and any discs provided by the manufacturer of your printer.

The following work must be carried out on all of the machines which do not have a printer directly connected.

Open up the **Printers** folder from **Start**, **Settings** and **Printers**. You will probably find the folder is empty apart from the **Add Printer** icon.

Double click the icon to start the **Add Printer Wizard** described over the page.

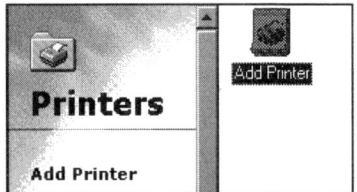

Click **Next** to leave the initial screen and on the dialogue box which
follows switch on the radio button to select **Network printer**. The next
window requires us to browse for the path to the network printer.

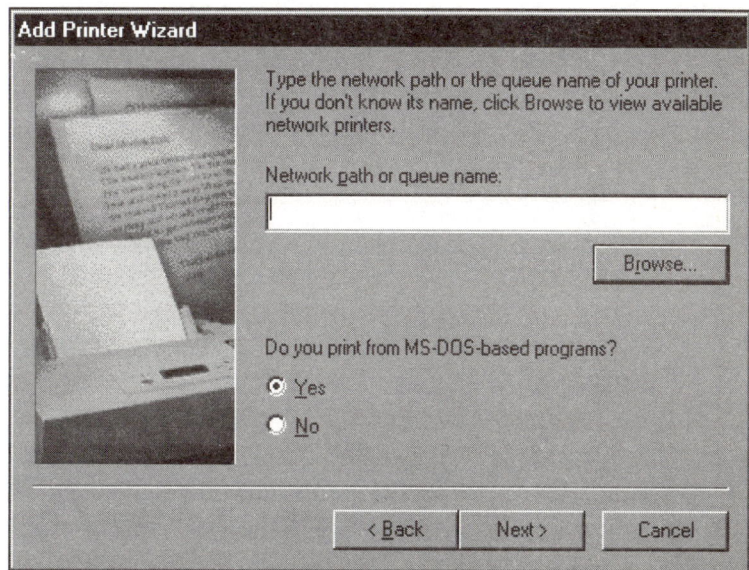

Selecting **Browse...** takes you into the **Network Neighbourhood**
where you can select the path of the machine to which the printer is
attached. Clicking on the icon for this machine (in my example, **Kestrel**)
should reveal the attached printer.

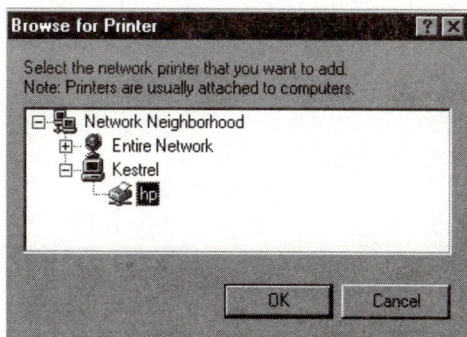

If you now click **OK** you should see the path to the printer displayed in the **Add Printer Wizard**.

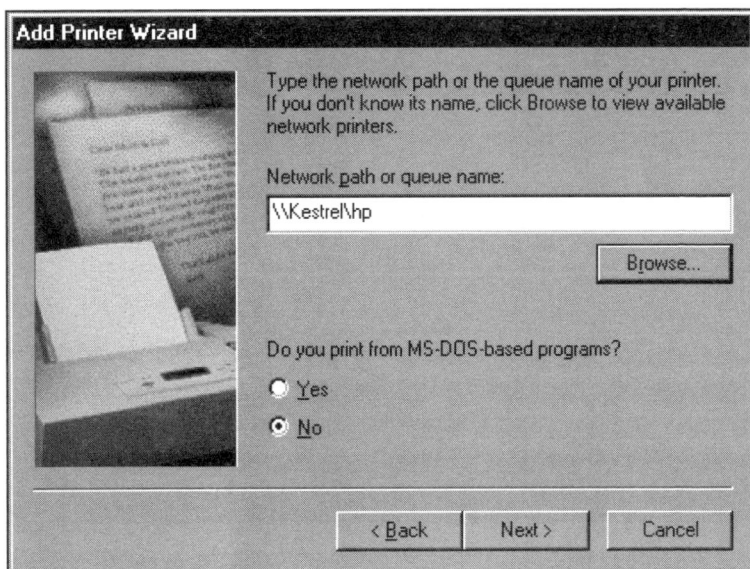

Before leaving this part of the **Add Printer Wizard** you have to switch on a radio button in answer to the question **Do you print from MSDOS-based programs?** If you select **Yes** you need to carry out an additional step to associate the network printer with the LPT (printer) port.

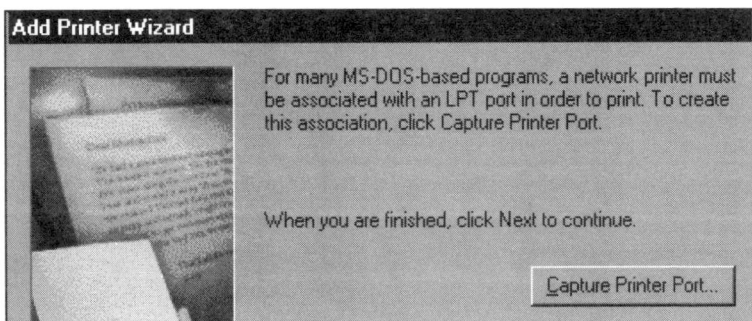

Now click the button **Capture Printer Port…**. The **Capture Printer Port** window appears, allowing you to select the **Device:** from the drop down menu. This is usually LPT1.

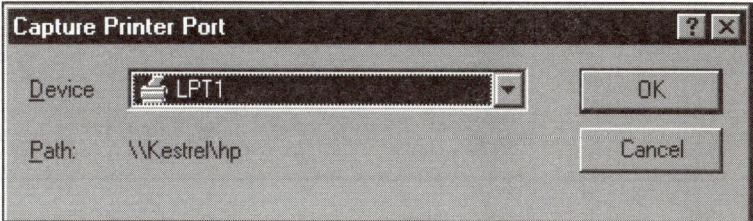

Capture Printer Port		? ☒
Device	🖨 LPT1 ▼	OK
Path:	\\Kestrel\hp	Cancel

If you select **No** to the question **Do you print from MSDOS-based programs?**, the previous procedure to capture a printer port is omitted.

From now on the procedure for adding the shared network printer to a workstation is the same whether you selected **Yes** or **No** to print from MSDOS-based programs.

You are presented with a dialogue box listing well-known brands of printer. If your printer appears on the list, select the make and model, then make sure your Windows 98 CD is in the drive and select **Next**.

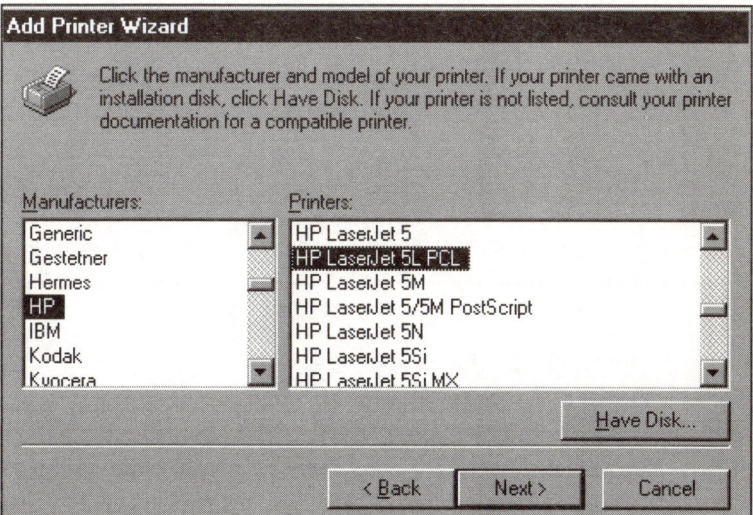

Add Printer Wizard

Click the manufacturer and model of your printer. If your printer came with an installation disk, click Have Disk. If your printer is not listed, consult your printer documentation for a compatible printer.

Manufacturers:	Printers:
Generic	HP LaserJet 5
Gestetner	HP LaserJet 5L PCL
Hermes	HP LaserJet 5M
HP	HP LaserJet 5/5M PostScript
IBM	HP LaserJet 5N
Kodak	HP LaserJet 5Si
Kyocera	HP LaserJet 5Si MX

Have Disk...

< Back   Next >   Cancel

Alternatively, if you have a less well-known printer which is not listed in the **Add Printer Wizard** shown previously you will need to click **Have Disk...** and insert the disc(s) provided by the manufacturer of your printer.

You are then given the opportunity to alter the supplied name for the printer and to print a *test page*.

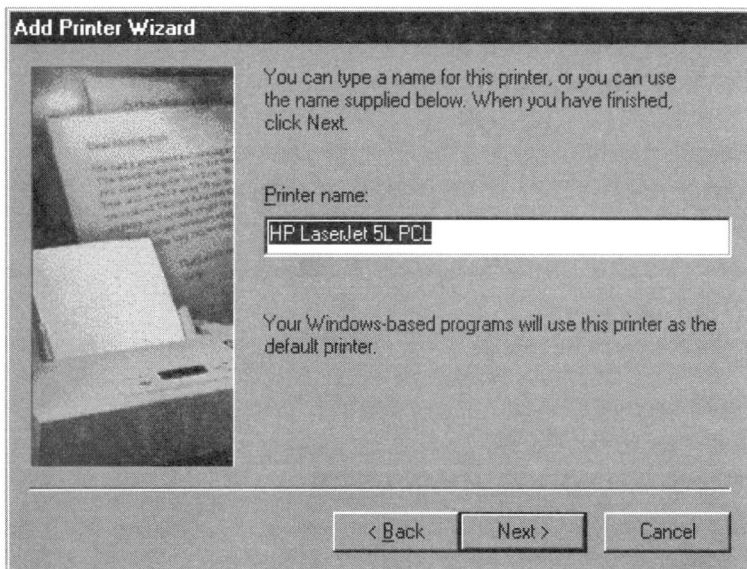

Clicking **Finish** copies any necessary files from the Windows 98 and prints a test page, if requested.

You are then asked if the page printed correctly. If the answer is **Yes** then the workstation is now set up to use the remote network printer. When you print from an application such as Word or Excel, the familiar **Print** dialogue box appears. Instead of the line **Where: LPT1** for a local printer the dialogue box displays **Where: \\Kestrel\hp**, the path for the network printer as shown on the next page.

From the **Print** dialogue box you can control the printing process just as if the remote network printer were directly attached to your machine.

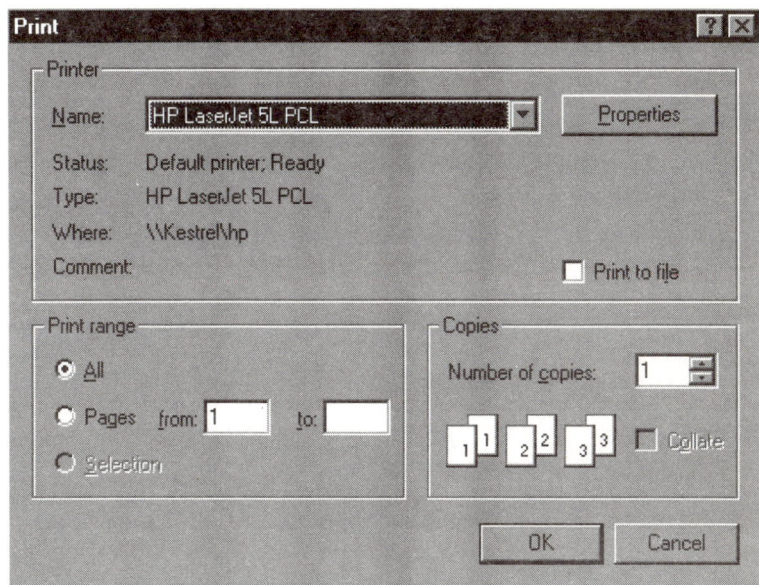

If the test print failed you are directed to the **Print Troubleshooter** which enables the diagnosing and solving of any problems.

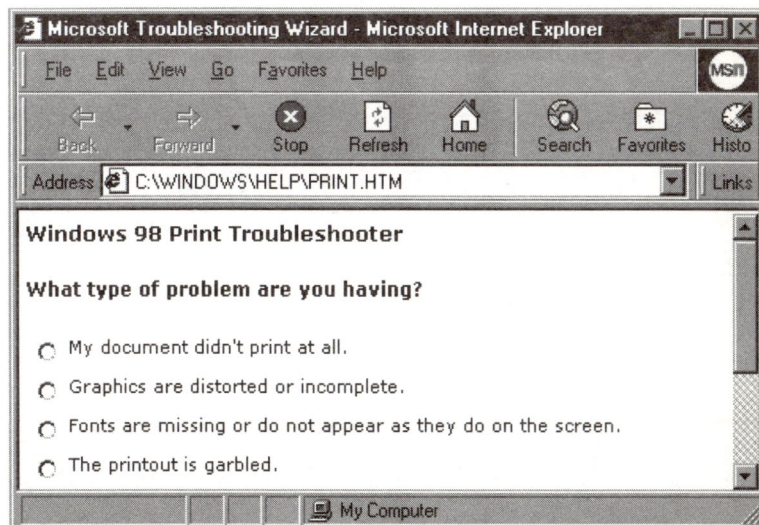

Summary: The Network Neighborhood

- All of the computers connected to the network are shown in the Network Neighborhood.

- Each computer and its shareable resources can be viewed in its own window on every workstation on the network.

- Copying files and folders can be carried out quickly and simply by "dragging and dropping" between the windows of different computers, displayed simultaneously on the screen.

- Drive mappings allow resources such as folders, disc drives, CD drives and ZIP drives to be represented by a single letter, such as **K:**. The mapped resource is then available to all of the workstations on the network, used in the same way as a local drive such as **A:**, **C:** or **D:**.

- Drive mappings can be created or removed in the **Windows Explorer**.

- In order to share a single network printer, each workstation must be individually set up using the **Add Printer Wizard** invoked from **Start**, **Settings**, **Printers** and **Add Printer**.

- The network printer can be used across the network from each workstation in the same way as a local printer directly attached to the workstation, using **File** and **Print** from applications such as Word.

Managing the Network

Net Watcher

This is a component within Windows 98 which allows you to administer the shared resources and users on the network. Working remotely at any of the workstations on the network, you can:

- Monitor who is using shared resources such as files and folders.
- Make new resources shareable or remove the sharing facility.
- Disconnect users from a shared resource.
- Administer a workstation remotely.

Net Watcher is supplied on the Windows 98 CD but it may not be installed on your computer because it's an optional component. You can check this by selecting **Start**, **Programs**, **Accessories** and **System Tools**. Net Watcher should appear on the resulting menu:

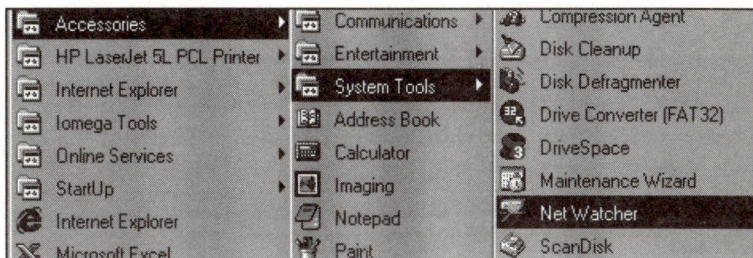

Installing Net Watcher

If Net Watcher doesn't appear on the menu system as previously described, you will need to carry out the installation from your Windows 98 CD. Select **Start**, **Settings**, **Control Panel** and double-click the **Add/Remove Programs** icon. Then select the **Windows Setup** tab and **System Tools**. Click the **Details...** button to reveal the list of **System Tools** components which have already been installed. Make sure a tick appears in the box next to **Net Watcher**.

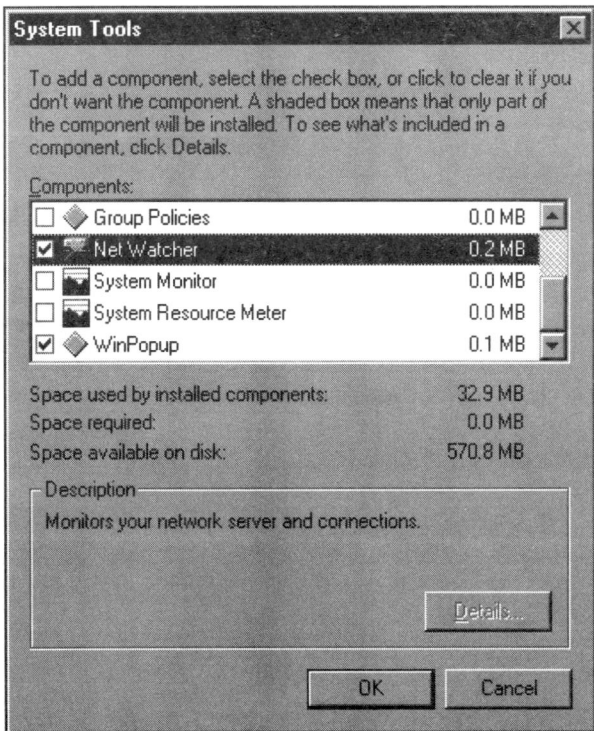

After you click **OK** you will be asked to insert your Windows 98 CD in the drive so that the necessary files can be copied to your hard disc.

Before you can use **Net Watcher**, your network must be working correctly with all of the workstations appearing in the **Network Neighborhood** as previously described. File and printer sharing must be enabled and **Client for Microsoft Networks** should be installed.

For a simple network of a few computers (rather than a large one with a network administrator) **Share-level access control** should be selected. This is switched on in the **Access Control** tab of the **Network** dialogue box accessed by double-clicking its icon in the **Control Panel** (**Start / Settings / Control Panel**).

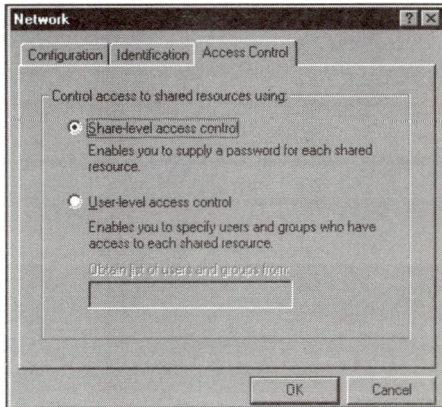

You must also enable **Re-mote Administration** on all of the workstations on the network. This is switched on by ticking the box on the **Remote Ad-ministration** tab, obtained by selecting **Start**, **Set-tings**, **Control Panel** and double-clicking the **Pass-words** icon. You must also enter and confirm a password.

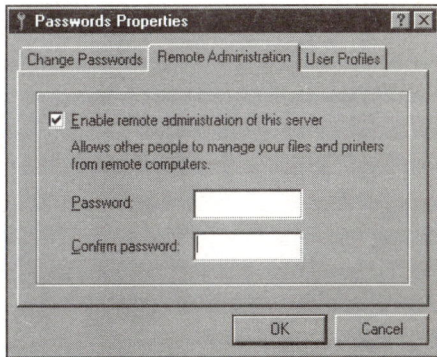

Using Net Watcher

The program can be invoked from within the **Network Neighborhood**. Highlight the workstation you wish to manage remotely then click the right button over its name.

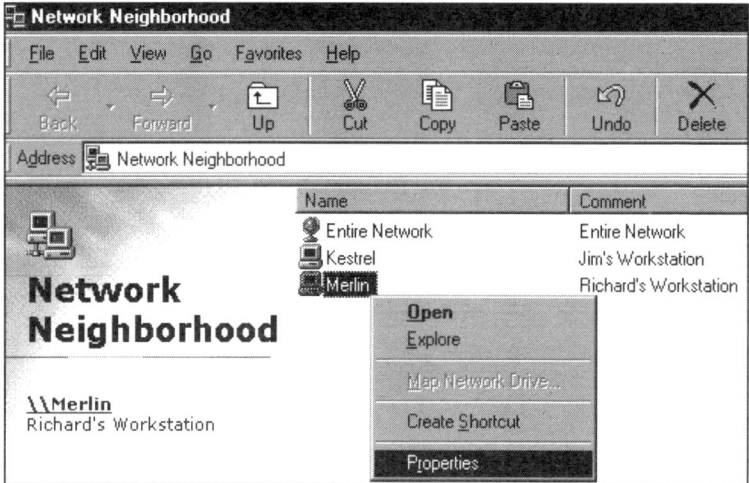

In this case I am choosing to remotely manage the **Merlin** computer while working at the **Kestrel**. Now select **Properties** and the **Tools** tab. This contains the buttons to start **Net Watcher** and to **Administer** the remote computer. (The **System Monitor** feature is not available with the **Share-level access control** used in this simple peer-to-peer network.)

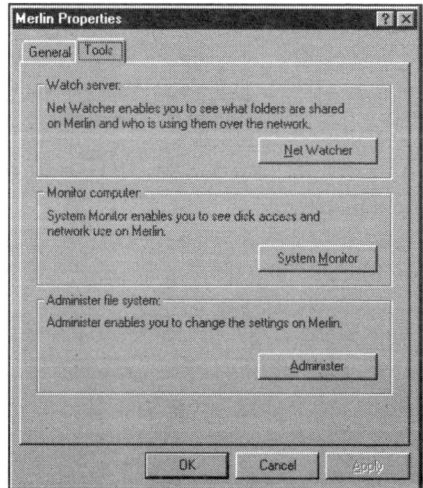

Selecting the **Net Watcher** button opens up the main window showing the user(s) and machine(s) connected to machine **MERLIN**.

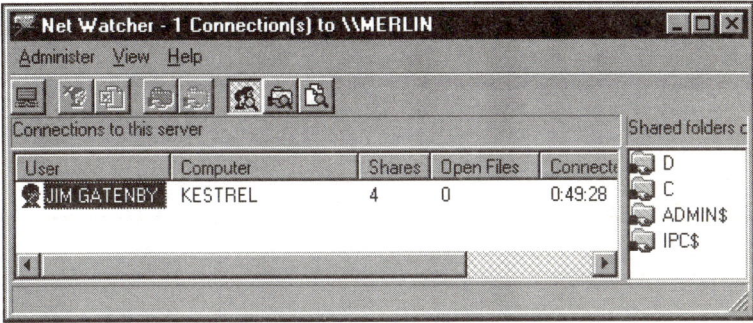

Alternatively you can start Net Watcher from the Windows 98 menu system as described previously, using **Start**, **Programs**, **Accessories**, **System Tools**, and **Net Watcher**. However, invoking Net Watcher in this way presents you with a blank window. You then need to click **Administer** and **Select Server...** from the menu bar.

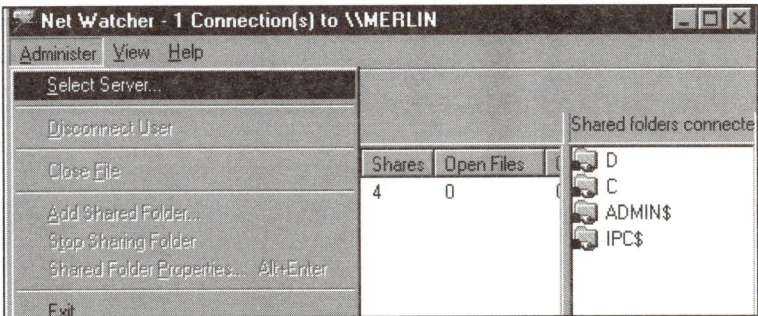

In our context, the term "server" just means the particular computer or workstation in the **Network Neighborhood** which we wish to administer remotely. In large organisations the server is a powerful computer at the centre of a network, used to manage the network and its users and store most of the software and data files. On our simple peer-to-peer network all workstations have equal status.

When you click **Select Server...** from the **Administer** menu in **Net Watcher** you are given the chance to type in the name of the machine you wish to administer.

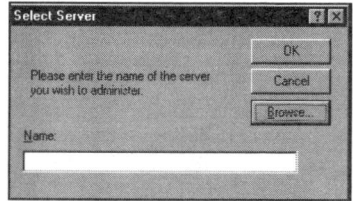

If you are unsure of the name of the workstation, selecting **Browse...** enables the required machine to be highlighted in the **Network Neighborhood**. Click **OK** to bring up the details of the remote machine in **Net Watcher** as shown previously.

Net Watcher can be operated by a group of icons along the menu bar or by drop down menus invoked from **Administer** and **View**.

Reading from left to right, the functions represented by the icons are:

- Select server
- Disconnect user
- Close file
- Add share
- Stop sharing
- Show users
- Show shared folders
- Show files

Alternatively, you can run Net Watcher from the drop down menus accessed from the menu bar. The **View** menu is shown below:

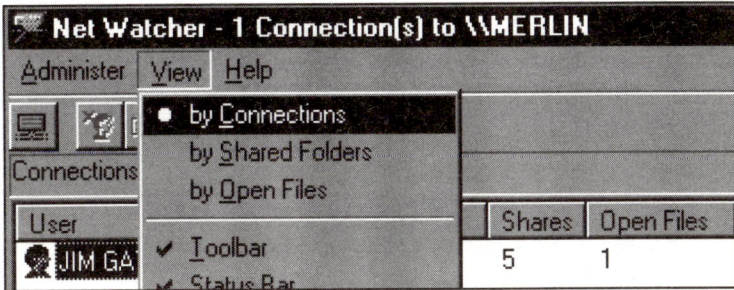

If you select **by Connections** from the **View** menu or the **Show Users** icon you can see who is accessing the remote computer, for how long and which computer they are working at.

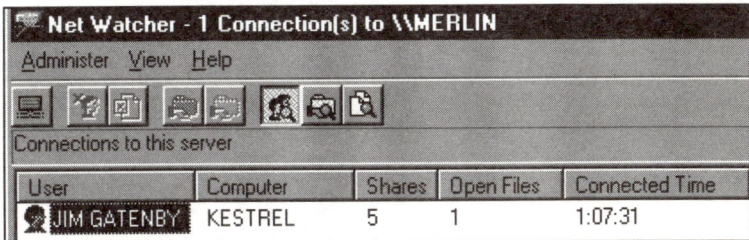

Clicking **by Shared Folders** from the **View** menu or clicking the **Show Shared folders** icon enables you to see which folders are shareable on the remote machine, which workstation is accessing them and the path to any shared files which have been opened.

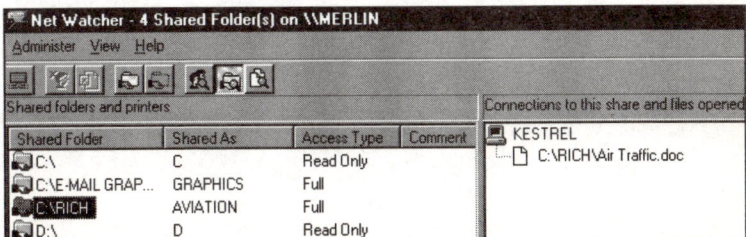

The **Administer** menu in Net Watcher allows you to carry out a number of operations on shared folders.

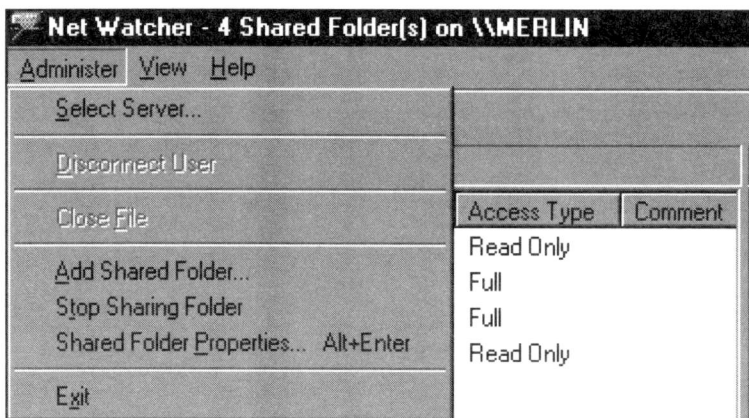

If you choose **Add Shared Folder...** you can enter the path to the folder to be shared, if you know it.

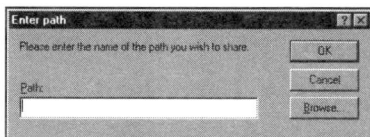

Alternatively if you select **Browse...**, Net Watcher allows you to make a choice from the   folders on the remote machine. When you select a new folder to make shareable and click **OK** you are presented with the **Shared   Folder   Proper-ties...** dialogue box which allows you to switch on sharing and add a name and password(s) for the shared folder.

The previously shown **Shared Folder Properties** dialogue box is also accessible from the **Administer** drop down menu from where you can also switch off the shareable property of a selected folder.

Returning to the **Properties** window for the remote machine **Merlin** shown earlier, the **Administer** button allows you to manage the file system of the remote workstation. This includes the full range of file and folder management activities such as deleting and renaming. You can also run **Windows Explorer** on the remote machine.

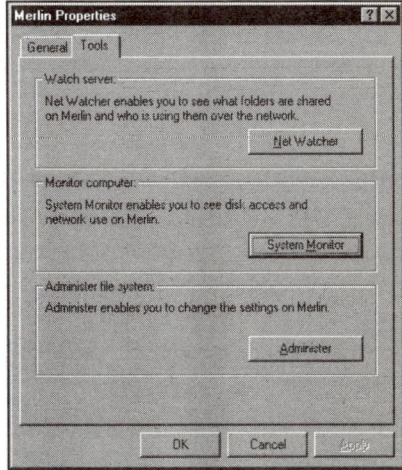

Merlin Properties dialog box

General | Tools

Watch server:
Net Watcher enables you to see what folders are shared on Merlin and who is using them over the network.

Net Watcher

Monitor computer:
System Monitor enables you to see disk access and network use on Merlin.

System Monitor

Administer file system:
Administer enables you to change the settings on Merlin.

Administer

OK | Cancel | Apply

WinPopup

When your network is up and running you may need to communicate with other people who are not within speaking distance - in another room in the house perhaps or in a different part of a business. Windows 98 includes the utility WinPopup which allows the sending and receiving of short text messages. WinPopup is supplied on the original Windows 98 CD but may not have been included in the list of optional components when Windows 98 was installed on your machine. You can see if WinPopup is installed by selecting **Start**, **Settings**, **Control Panel** and double-clicking on the **Add/Remove Programs** icon. Select the **Windows Setup** tab, scroll down to **System Tools** and click **Details....**

WinPopup window: Messages Help

You should see a tick in the box next to **WinPopup**. Make sure WinPopup is ticked and click **OK**. If necessary, you will be asked to insert your Windows 98 CD so that the essential files can be copied.

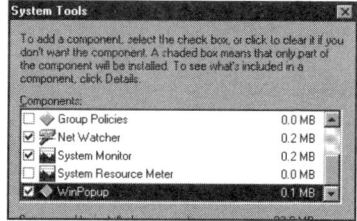

Once installed, WinPopup can be invoked by selecting **Start** and **Run...** and entering its name in the **Open:** bar.

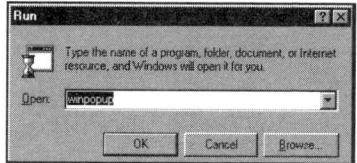

Wokstations which are to receive messages must have WinPopup already running - unobtrusively minimised on the taskbar. To send a message, first click the icon representing an envelope.

This opens a window in which you can type a short message. The radio button **To:** allows messages to be sent either to a named user or computer on the network or to everyone in a particular workgroup.

After entering the text, click **OK** and you should be informed that the message was successfully sent. The recipient workstation(s) may emit a beep (optional) to announce the arrival of the message as it pops up in its own window on the screen.

An optional dialogue across the top of the message window gives the sender, the date and the time. There are buttons to scroll through the accumulated messages and an icon for deleting messages.

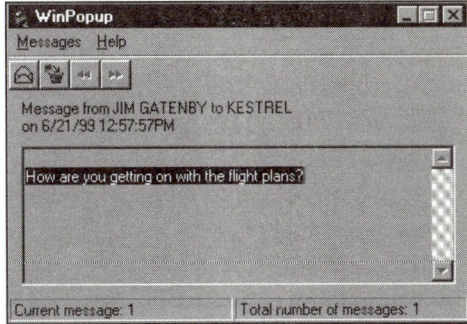

WinPopup can also be operated by clicking **Messages** on the menu bar. This includes options to **Send...** new messages and manage existing ones.

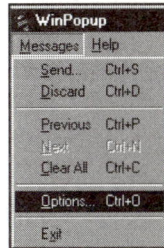

Options... allows you to specify the way a message is announced and displayed when it arrives at its destination.

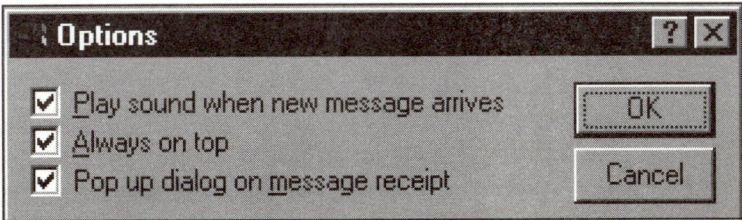

Starting WinPopup Automatically

To receive messages, all workstations must have WinPopup currently up and running, probably minimised on the taskbar. If you wish to have WinPopup running every time Windows 98 starts up, it must be included in the **StartUp** folder. This is achieved by selecting **Start, Settings, Taskbar and Start Menu....** Select the **Start Menu Programs** tab, click **Add...** then **Browse....**

You need to locate **Win-Popup.exe** - it should be in the **Windows** folder. Click the file name and **Open** to place the path to Win-Popup in the **Create Shortcut** dialogue box. Click **Next** and then double-click the **Startup** folder. Enter the name to appear on the **Startup** menu and then click **Finish**. WinPopup should now run automatically whenever the computer starts up.

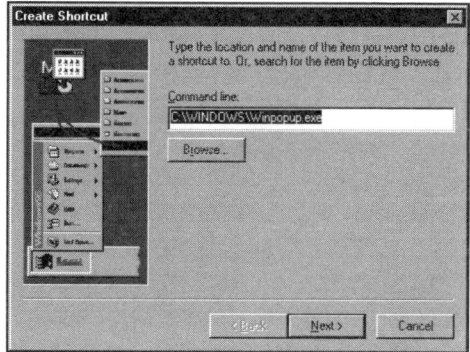

Summary: Managing the Network

- Net Watcher is a component of Windows 98 and enables you to remotely manage the shared resources on a network. The software may need to be installed from the original Windows 98 CD using **Windows Setup**.

- Workstations to be managed must have **Remote Administration** enabled in the **Passwords** facility of the **Control Panel**.

- Net Watcher can be started from the **Programs** menu in **Accessories**/**System Tools** or from the **Properties/Tools** window in the **Network Neighborhood**.

- Sharing of resources can be enabled or terminated using Net Watcher, and *users* can be disconnected.

- The **Administer** feature allows you to manage the *filing system* and change settings on a remote computer.

- WinPopup is a Windows 98 utility which allows short messages to be sent to individual computers or entire workgroups on the network.

- In order that messages can be received around the network, WinPopup must be running on the workstations. This can be automated by placing WinPopup in the **Startup** folder.

Sharing the Internet

Introduction

One of the most compelling reasons for networking several computers in the home or small business must be to give more people access to the Internet. At the same time, two or more members of a household may want to surf the net or use an e-mail application such as Outlook Express. One solution would be to install an extra telephone line and run each machine independently, with its own modem. However, this is expensive, involving telephone installation costs, line rental charges and additional wiring around the home or business premises. Artisoft Inc. of Tucson Arizona have developed a number of products which allow networked computers to share a single Internet connection, modem and telephone line. These are *software* solutions and cheaper than the hardware alternative - a device called a *router*, which is also more complex to set up and manage.

i.Share 3.0 allows up to 32 users on a network to share *simultaneously* a single Internet connection via one modem and telephone line. Individual workstations can access the Internet using their Web browser, as if there was a modem directly attached to their machine. i.Share works by allowing multiple computers to share the Winsock software; this is part of Windows 98, which enables your computer to communicate with the Internet using the TCP/IP protocol (language).

ModemShare 32 is a related product from Artisoft which allows each computer on a network to use (one at a time), a modem and all of its facilities (not just the Internet) including the sending of faxes and connecting to bulletin boards.

Artisoft Inc. is represented for sales and technical support in the United Kingdom by Redycrest Ltd. Information about Artisoft Products and downloads from the Internet are available from:

www.artisoft.co.uk

www.artisoft.com

Complete evaluation versions of the software may be downloaded free from www.artisoft.com. If you *purchase* (rather than *download*) the software, you are provided with a serial number and a verification key to be entered during the installation process. You can choose to leave the entries for serial number and verification key blank during the setup process. In this case your installation of i.Share 3.0 will be an *evaluation copy* only, which terminates after 30 days. You can, however, buy a serial number and verification key from Artisoft at a later date, and upgrade your evaluation copy to an unrestricted version.

The methods of obtaining and installing i.Share 3.0 and ModemShare 32 are very similar. To avoid repetition, only the installation of i.Share 3.0 is described in the remainder of this chapter.

i.Share 3.0

i.Share works by making a single Internet connection shareable by two or more computers (up to a maximum of 32 machines). The computer which has the modem directly attached is known as the *Server*. The workstations around the network which will share the Internet connection are known as *Clients*. The Server must be set up with a working modem and dial-up connection to the Internet. The Client machines must have an Internet browser such as Internet Explorer, set to "*connect to the Internet across a local area network*". The downloaded file contains both the Client and Server software. The setup procedure is very similar for both Client and Server machines.

Data and information received from the Internet arrives at the i.Share Server in the TCP/IP protocol - the language of the Internet. It's then translated to the NetBEUI protocol used for communication with the various Client workstations around the network.

i.Share and ModemShare can be bought on CD from computer shops and by mail order. You can also try it free by downloading an evaluation copy from the Internet. This is a complete working copy but it only works for 30 days unless you upgrade by buying a serial number and verification key. The overall process to get i.Share up and running on your network is as follows:

- Working at your *Server* machine (the one with the modem attached), log on to the Artisoft Web site.

- Download the software to your hard disc as a compressed Zip file.

- Extract the compressed file and install the i.Share Server software on your *Server* machine.

- Moving to a *Client* machine start the **Network Neighborhood** and open up (on the Client screen) the window showing the shareable resources for the Server machine.

- Working at the Client, in Network Neighborhood, locate the downloaded i.Share software in its folder on the hard disc of your Server machine. (This will need to be *shareable* as described in previous chapters).

- Still working at the Client machine, install the i.Share software from the Server machine across the network to the Client machine.

- Repeat the process for all of the Client computers on your network.

Downloading i.Share 3.0

Log on to the Artisoft Web site and select the **Download** button. From the drop-down list select i.Share 3.0 and fill in the few personal details required such as your name, telephone number and e-mail address. Now click **Submit** and select to download the English version. After accepting **Save this program to disk** you are given the opportunity to select which folder the downloaded program file will be copied into on your hard disc. Make a note of this folder.

In this example I had already created a folder, **i.Share**, in which to store the downloaded file. Note that the file to be downloaded is a self-extracting ZIP file called **is30eval.exe**. This is a file which has been compressed using a program like WinZip, in order to speed the download process.

The **.exe** extension at the end of the file name means it can unzip itself without the presence of a copy of a file compression/extraction program such as WinZip or PKUNZIP.

Once you click **Save**, the download from the Internet begins and a window on the screen informs you of progress. The download process for i.Share 3.0 took about 10 minutes on my computer.

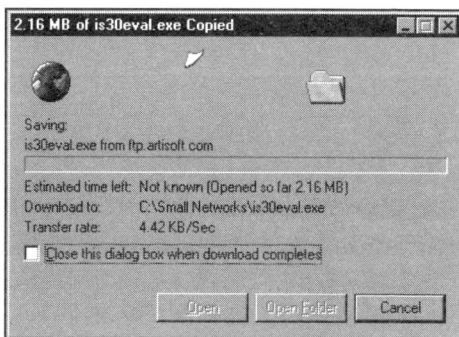

At the end of the download process you have the compressed file **is30eval.exe** stored in the folder of your choice. This can be confirmed by locating it in the **Windows Explorer** or **My Computer**.

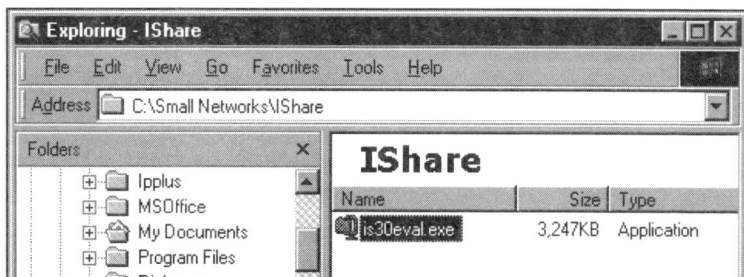

Now double-click the name of the file, **is30eval.exe**, and click **Unzip** on the resulting **WinZip Self-Extractor** dialogue box. This extracts the compressed file to produce the i.Share setup file.

Installing i.Share Server

By default the i.Share setup program will start automatically as soon as the unzipping is finished. This can be switched off by unticking the check box **When Done UnzippingRun:**... To set up i.Share, you must then run

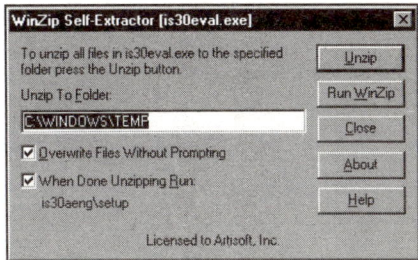

manually the program, **is30aeng\setup**, from whatever folder it's been unzipped into (**C:\WINDOWS\TEMP** by default).

During the setup program you are asked to enter your **Serial Number** and **Verification Key**.

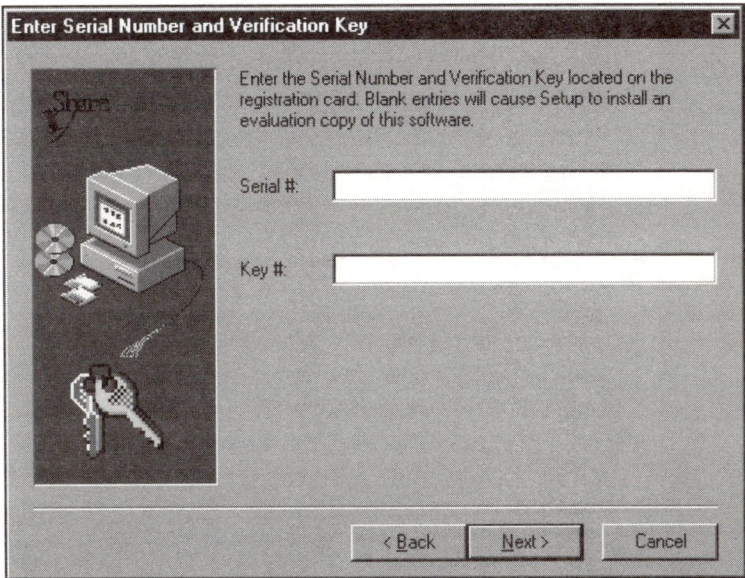

Leave these blank and i.Share will be installed as a 30-day evaluation copy. If you purchase i.Share at a later date, you will be supplied with the necessary details to upgrade i.Share to an unrestricted copy.

After accepting (or otherwise) the various default settings such as the folders into which i.Share will be installed, you need to select the type of network you are using. In our small peer-to-peer network based on Windows 98, the type of network is **NetBEUI**.

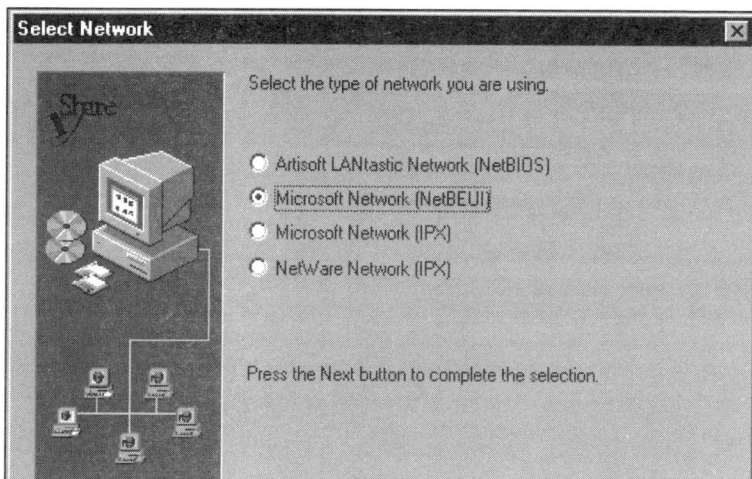

The next dialogue box allows us to specify that we want to set up the i.Share *Server* software.

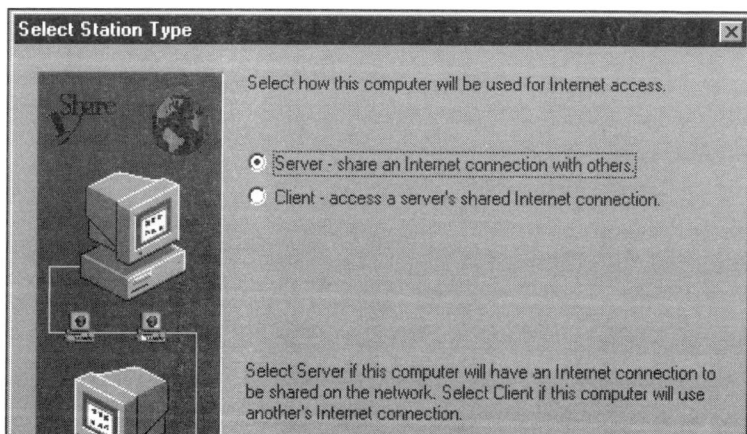

Next you are given the opportunity to enter a name which the Server computer will be known as when Clients connect using i.Share.

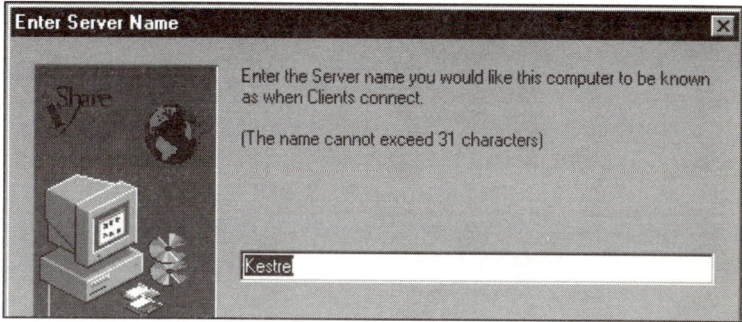

By default this will be the name you provided previously for **Computer Name:** in the **Identification** tab of the **Network** window, which is accessed from **Start**, **Settings**, **Control Panel** and the **Network** icon.

If you now click **Next** you are given the chance to confirm or redo the settings you have entered. Then the i.Share program files are copied to your hard disc. You need to restart the computer to complete the installation. When i.Share Server is working to provide shared access for the workstations around the network you don't actually need to start it up like a normal application. i.Share starts up automatically when you launch an Internet application such as Internet Explorer from a workstation. i.Share Server runs unseen in the background but its presence is shown by an icon on the taskbar at the bottom right of the screen.

Clicking this icon allows you to use i.Share Server to carry out management tasks such as preventing access to certain Web sites using **i.Watch** (discussed later). i.Share Server can also be launched using **Start**, **Programs** and **i.Share**.

Installing i.Share Client

The basic process is the same as the setting up of i.Share Server described previously. However, the fact that the downloaded file containing the i.Share setup program is on the Server machine enables us to make use of our small network. Working at a Client machine, we simply locate the setup program in the Network Neighborhood in the window for the Server computer. Then we run the set up program from the Client machine.

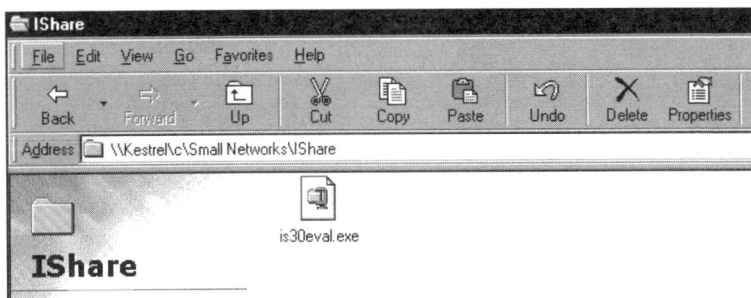

Double clicking on the icon for **is30evl.exe** starts the process to extract the Zip file and begin the installation process for i.Share Client. The procedure is almost identical to the installation of i.Share Server, the only difference being the need to select **Client - access a Server's shared Internet connection** as shown below. Once the files are copied you are asked to restart the computer.

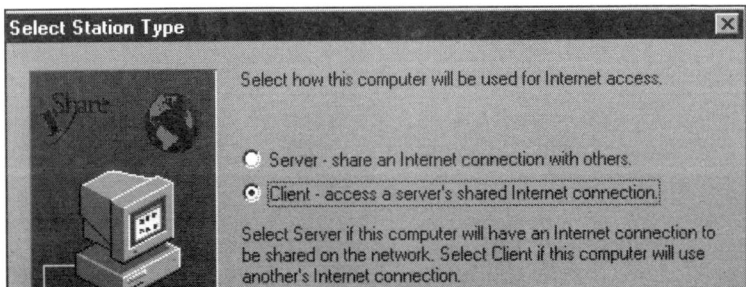

i.Share Client

i.Share Client runs in the background with a globe icon on the bottom right of the toolbar.

You can launch it on the screen from **Start**, **Programs** and **i.Share**.

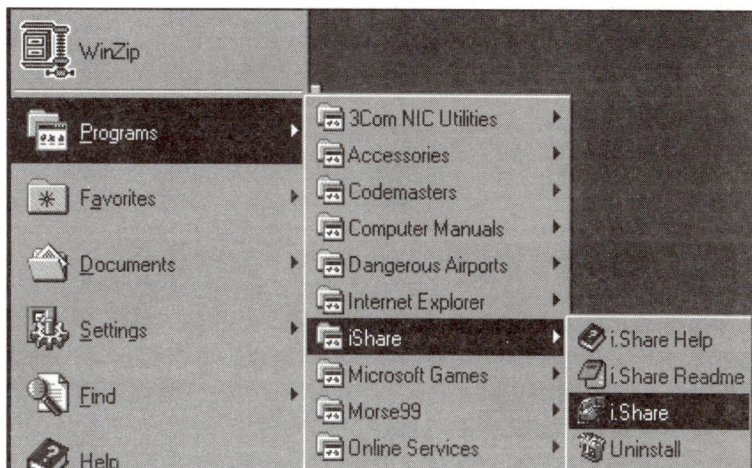

However, you don't need to see i.Share Client running on the screen unless you want to change some of the settings. Normally the user will simply start their browser, such as Internet Explorer, and connect to the Internet without seeing i.Share Server working in the background. All dialling is done by the Server machine. If any of the Client machines on your network have previously been set up with their own modem you need to make sure they don't try to dial independently. For example in the Internet Explorer, right-click its icon on the Windows 98 desktop, and select **Properties** and the **Connections** tab. Make sure the browsers in the Client machines are set to **Connect to the Internet using a local area net-work**, rather than using a modem.

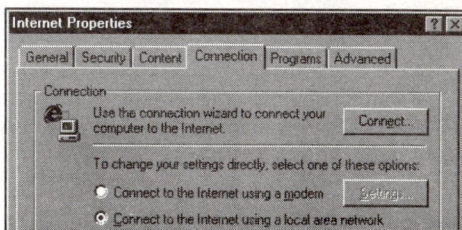

As already stated, using i.Share to connect to the Internet from a Client (or Server), should be virtually seamless, except for the icons running on the right-hand side of the Windows 98 taskbar. However, you may wish to look at the **i.Share Connection Manager** at a Client by clicking the globe icon on the taskbar (or using **Start**, **Programs**, **i.Share** or double-clicking its icon in the **Control Panel**).

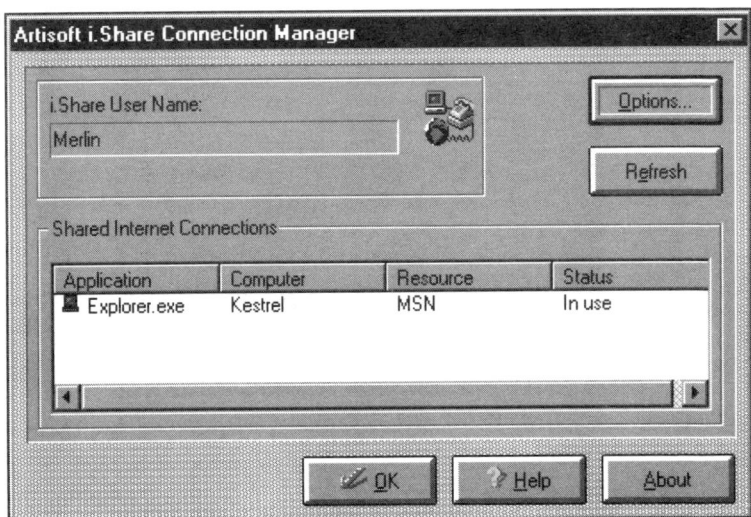

The **Connection Manager** shows the name of the Client computer, in this case **Merlin,** and this can be changed after clicking the **Options** button. The window above also shows that the Client is connected using the Internet Explorer application, **Explorer.exe**. **Kestrel** under the **Computer** heading refers to the Server computer which is making the modem connection to the Internet and the **Resource,** in this case **MSN**, is the shared Internet account. There are also various options for the way resources are selected (in the case of networks with multiple Servers). The **Status** column currently showing **In use** might, in other circumstances, show **Server not found** or **Resource not found**.

i.Share Server

This is the program used to manage the Internet sharing system. It can be launched, as previously described, by clicking its icon on the Windows 98 taskbar, from **Start**, **Programs** and **i.Share** or from **Start**, **Settings**, **Control Panel** and double-clicking its icon.

The main **i.Share Server** window open at the **Status** tab is shown below. This monitors the use of the system and gives details of the users.

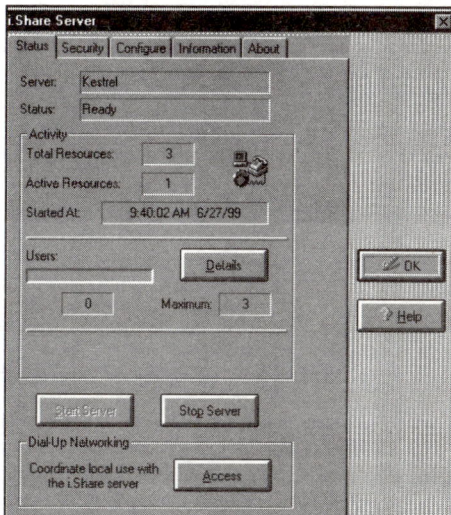

The name of the i.Share Server computer can be changed after clicking the **Configure** tab. This name can, if you wish, be different from the network identification name assigned to the computer, as described earlier in this book. The **Status** tab above shows the time the Server was started and gives the option to terminate sharing by clicking **Stop Server**. The **Details** button provides information about Clients activities in the sharing of the network. This includes the name of the Client machine, the amount of data (bytes) sent and received and an option to disconnect the user.

Security

You can control access to individual Web sites using **i.Watch**, which is entered from its button on the security tab in **i.Share Server**.

You can permit or prevent entry to all sites (other than those listed) by ticking or leaving blank the check box **Allow access to all other URLs**. This is located in the **i.Watch Restriction List** entered by clicking the **i.Watch** button in **i.Share Server**.

The URL list is compiled in **i.Share Server** by clicking **Security**, **i.Watch** and **Add** then entering the URL of the site(s) in the **i.Watch List** and setting the site as **Allowed** or **Disallowed**.

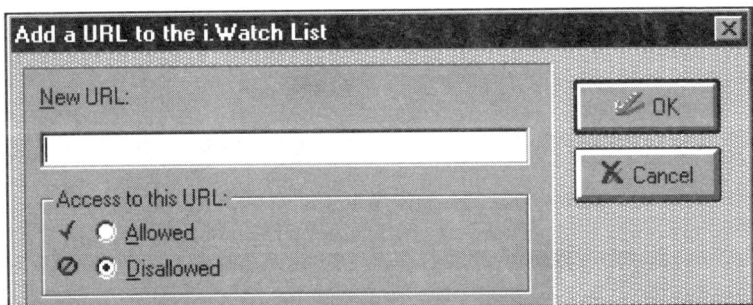

Sites can also be removed from the list and it is possible to **Import** and **Export** URLs using the comma separated variable (.CSV) format.

The Security tab in **i.Watch** also has a facility for adding passwords to i.Share resources (Internet connections). These may give either unrestricted access or access within the limits set in **i.Watch**.

ModemShare 32

ModemShare 32 is another program from Artisoft which allows all of the computers on a network to share a single modem and telephone line. However, whereas i.Share is dedicated to sharing a single Internet connection, ModemShare provides all of the facilities of the modem including fax, accessing bulletin boards as well as browsing the Internet. While i.Share allows several users to connect *simultaneously*, ModemShare only permits one machine on-line at a given time.

With both packages, the machine to which the modem is attached is designated as the Server while the workstations around the network are the Clients. ModemShare requires each Client machine to be set up with modem and communication software as if the modem were physically attached. (In the case of i.Share, only the Server makes the dial-up connection to the Internet Service Provider). Browser software such as Internet Explorer must be installed on each ModemShare Client and set to **Connect to the Internet using a modem.**

The process of downloading an evaluation copy and installing the ModemShare software is very similar to that described for i.Share. Again the evaluation copy is fully functioning for a limited period and the time restriction can be removed by purchasing and entering a Serial Number and Verification Key.   Client and Server are distinguished during the setup by ticking one or both of the boxes as shown below.

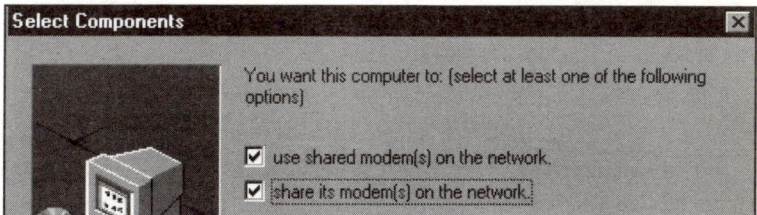

Once installed, each person on the network can use the modem as if it were directly attached to their computer.   When an Internet or fax program is launched this initiates a dial-up connection on the screen of the client, while ModemShare works unseen in the background.

Summary: Sharing the Internet

- i.Share 3.0 and ModemShare 32 are software products from Artisoft Inc., which allow several networked computers to use a single modem and telephone line.

- i.Share is dedicated to sharing an Internet connection *simultaneously* between several computers. ModemShare provides a full range of modem facilities (to one workstation at a time).

- Complete versions of the software may be downloaded from the Internet site **www.artisoft.com** and evaluated over a limited period of time.

- i.Share and ModemShare work on the *Client/Server* model, the server being the machine with the modem directly attached.

- The i.Share Server computer handles all of the dialling and Internet connections for the client machines, using the TCP/IP Internet protocol. Data is translated to the network protocol (e.g. NetBEUI) for communication with the various workstations.

- ModemShare client computers must be set up with their own dial-up connection and a modem "installed" in every client machine as if each client had a modem physically attached.

- Once installed, both i.Share and ModemShare run in the background, virtually unseen by the user. Normal Internet and fax applications such as Internet Explorer and Netscape Navigator are launched as if the user were working at a standalone machine with its own modem.

- i.Share Server has management facilities to monitor and control users. The i.Watch feature allows access to certain Web sites to be controlled by adding their URL to a restricted list. URLs may also be added to the restricted list by importing from other programs using the .CSV format. Access can be further controlled by the use of passwords.

Internet Connection Sharing

Introduction

The original version of Windows 98 made no provision for sharing a single Internet connection (using one modem and one telephone line) between several computers on a network. This need was filled by third-party products such as i.Share from Artisoft, described previously. However, at the time of writing Microsoft have just released Windows 98 Second Edition containing, amongst other things, Internet Connection Sharing. If you already have the first edition of Windows 98 you can obtain an upgrade CD after printing out an order form from:

www.microsoft.com/windows98

The total cost of the upgrade including postage is under £20. Alternatively if you've not yet purchased Windows 98 you will need to buy the full version of Windows 98 Second Edition.

The basic requirement is that you must have a functional network of two or more machines fitted with network interface cards and cabling. Creating a peer-to-peer network by installing network interface cards and cabling is covered elsewhere in this book. One of the machines, often referred to as the **Gateway** must be fitted with a modem or other means of connecting to the Internet. The Gateway machine on the Internet Connection Sharing network acts like a small scale version of one of the servers at the Internet Service Providers. The ordinary workstations on the network on which users browse the Internet will be referred to as **Clients**.

Before starting the process to install Internet Connection Sharing you should check that both the modem and the network are working correctly. Each of the Client machines needs a browser such as Internet Explorer installed. The browser or other Internet application such as Outlook Express must be set to connect to the Internet via a LAN (Local Area Network) - not by dialling independently via its own modem. All dialling is done by the modem attached to the Gateway computer. Once the system is up and running users of Client machines connect to the Internet by launching the browser in the normal way. The Client machines do not actually connect directly to the Internet. The Gateway machine processes requests for Internet information from the Clients and subsequently routes the answers back to them.   The Gateway machine and each Client machine are identified by an individual **IP Address**, a unique number such as **192.168.0.253** for example. These addresses are allocated by the Gateway machine.

Installing Internet Connection Sharing

TCP/IP

These are the protocols (Transmission Control Protocol/Internet Protocol) - the languages by which machines communicate on the Internet. TCP/IP is supplied as a component of Windows 98 and you need to make sure it's installed on all of the machines on the network. You can check by selecting **Start**, **Settings**, **Control Panel**, and **Network**.

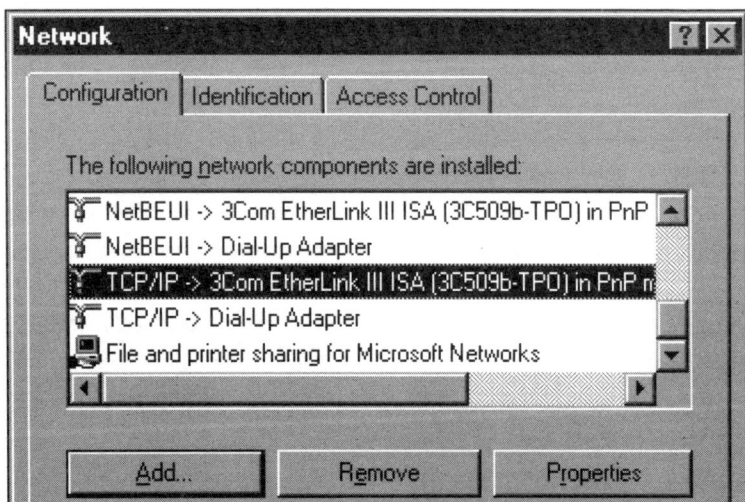

Scroll down the list of network components. If **TCP/IP** doesn't appear it will have to be installed using **Add...** and **Protocol** followed by **Add...** and **Microsoft**, before scrolling down to select **TCP/IP**. This process is described in more detail elsewhere in this book.

Then you need to set each machine on the network to obtain their IP addresses automatically.   This is done by highlighting the **TCP/IP** component in the **Network** dialogue box shown previously. (If there is more than one TCP/IP listed select   the one associated with the network adapter). Then click **Properties** and check that **Obtain an IP address automatically** is switched on.

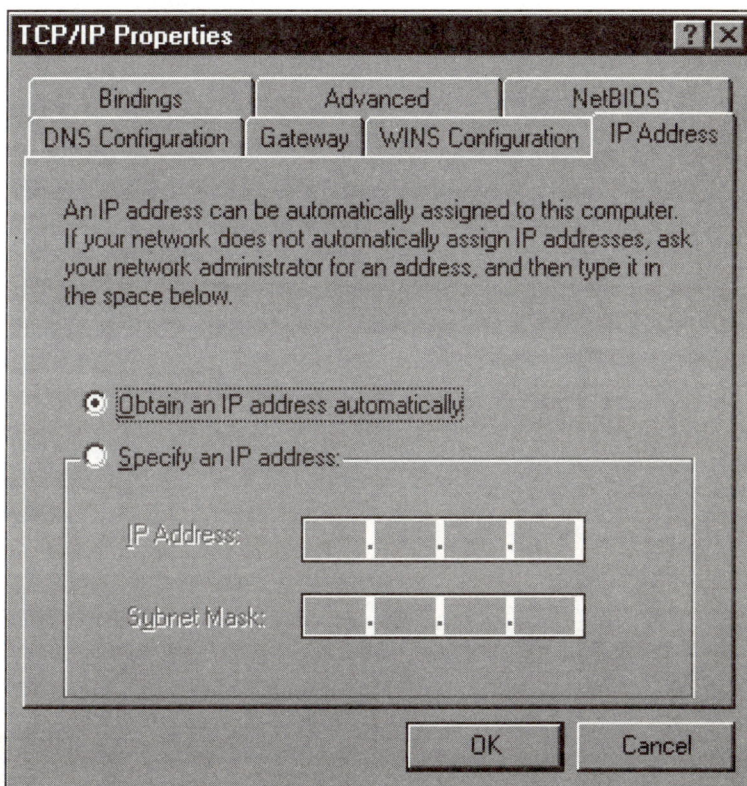

TCP/IP Properties   ? X

| Bindings | Advanced | NetBIOS |

| DNS Configuration | Gateway | WINS Configuration | IP Address |

An IP address can be automatically assigned to this computer.
If your network does not automatically assign IP addresses, ask
your network administrator for an address, and then type it in
the space below.

⦿ Obtain an IP address automatically

○ Specify an IP address:

IP Address: [.   .   .   ]

Subnet Mask: [.   .   .   ]

OK   Cancel

Now, still working with the **TCP/IP Properties** dialogue box:

- Click the **WINS Configuration** tab and select **Use DHCP for WINS Resolution**.
- Click the **Gateway** tab and remove any **Installed gateways:**.
- Click the **DNS Configuration** tab and select **Disable DNS**.
- Click **OK** and restart the computer so that these settings can take effect.

Setting Up the Gateway Computer

We need to ensure that the Windows 98 Second Edition component Internet Connection Sharing is installed on the Gateway machine - but not on the Clients. Working on the Gateway machine, select **Start**, **Settings**, **Control Panel**, **Add/Remove Programs** and click **Windows Setup**. Scroll down and select **Internet Tools** and click **Details....**

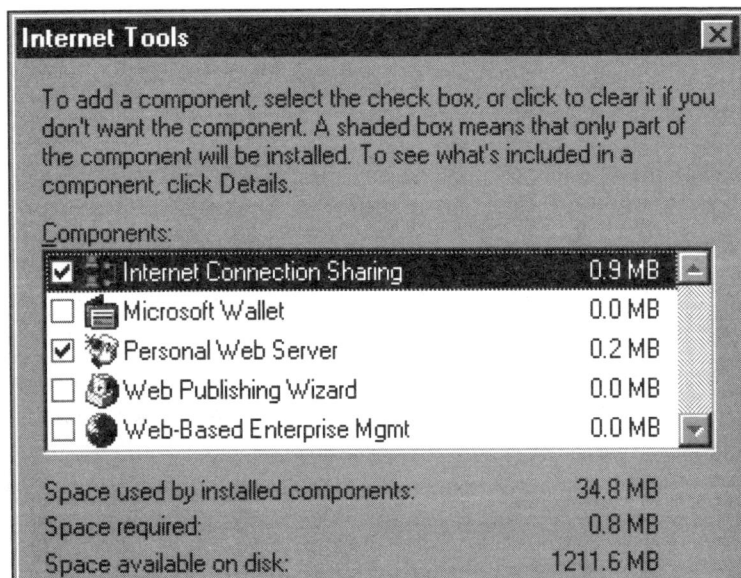

Make sure there is a tick next to **Internet Connection Sharing**.

Click **OK** and **Apply**. You will be asked to install the **Windows 98 Second Edition CD** so that the software can be copied. Then the **Internet Connection Sharing** wizard is launched.

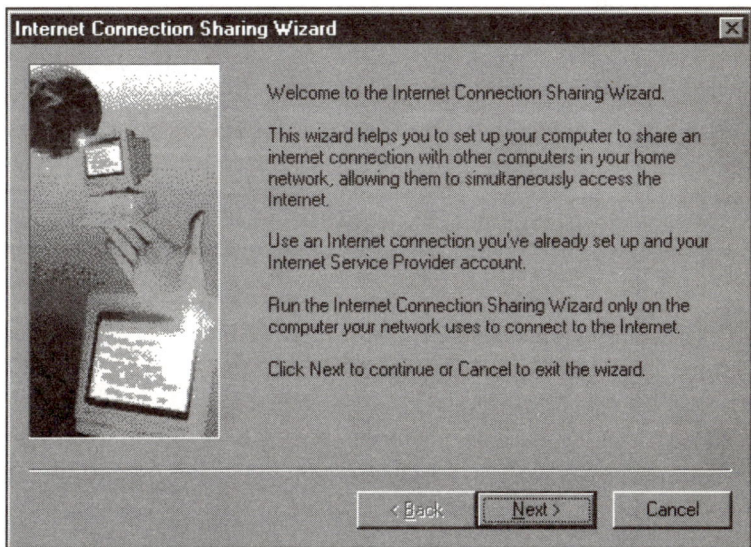

The wizard will ask you to provide a blank floppy disc so that a **Client Configuration Disk** can be created. After the disc has been created click **OK** then **Finish** and restart the computer to complete the setting up of the Gateway machine.

Setting Up the Client

The **Client Configuration Disk** must now be used on each of the Client machines in turn. The disc contains a setup program **icsclset.exe** and a text file **ReadMe.txt**. (The latter contains useful additional information about setting up Internet Connection Sharing. It's worth making a hard copy of **ReadMe.txt** after loading it into a program like Word or Notepad.) Before starting the Client setup process make sure the network is working correctly and the Gateway machine is connected online to the Internet.

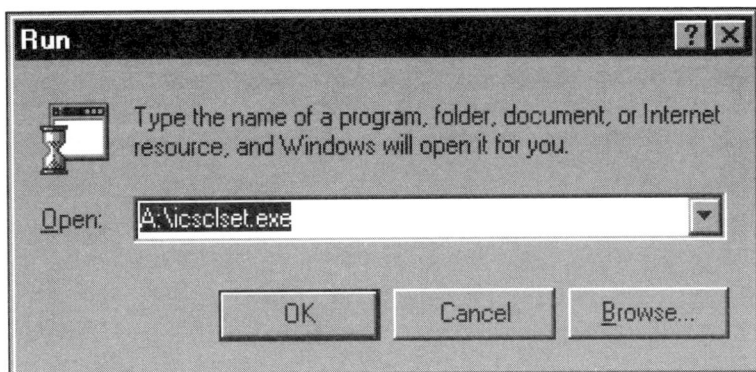

Place the floppy disc in the drive on the first Client machine and run **icslset.exe**.

This will start the **Browser Connection Setup Wizard** and also make sure that the Client is set to connect to the Internet over a local area network (LAN) rather than dialling with a modem. Working through the wizard mainly involves clicking **Next**.

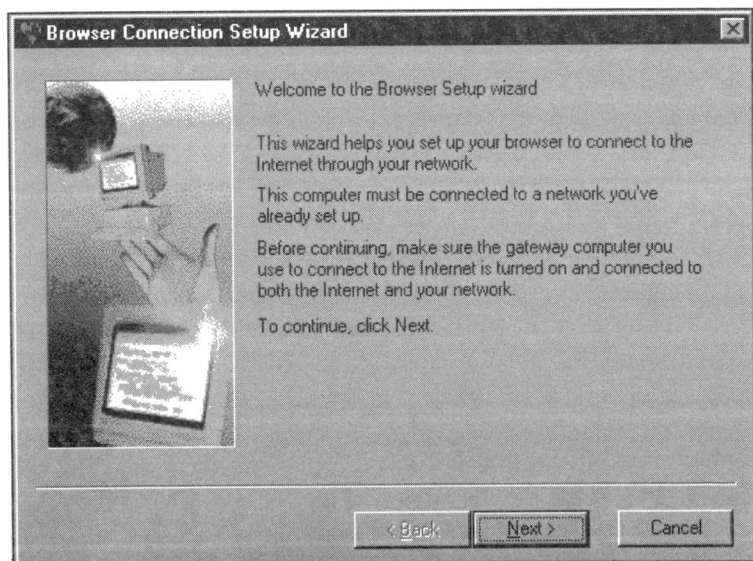

The Client setup process must be completed on all of the client machines on the network.

Making Connections

It doesn't matter whether the Gateway machine is online to the Internet or not when you try to connect from a Client machine. If the Gateway computer is already connected to the Internet, then getting online from a Client is quick and seamless. Just start up your browser such as Internet Explorer or other Internet application like Outlook Express. If the Gateway is not currently connected to the Internet, the Client will communicate with the Gateway machine across the LAN and quickly start the dialling process on the Gateway modem.

The Internet Connection Sharing system has worked well on my home network of two machines. It was simple to set up and two people can simultaneously browse the Web without any obvious degradation of performance. One slight issue is that after closing down a Client browser, the Gateway remains connected to the Internet ready for other clients to use. You may need to monitor this carefully and disconnect the Gateway machine separately if you are concerned about connection charges.

Investigating IP Addresses

Earlier it was mentioned that IP addresses would be allocated automatically. This task is done by the Gateway machine in a similar way to the server of your Internet Service Provider. Every time you log on to the Internet your Internet Service Provider gives your machine a different IP address - unless your system uses *static* rather than *dynamic* addressing.

The IP address is used by the Internet servers and your own Gateway machine to handle requests for Internet information from your browser and to route them back again.

The powerful server computers at the Internet Service Providers managing users and providing access to Web sites are also identified by unique IP numbers. This includes the Domain Name Servers (DNS) at the Internet Service Providers.

These servers contain lists which enable the translation of the *relatively* friendly URL names such as **www.enterprise.co.uk** into obscure IP addresses such as **192.168.0.2**.

If you are curious to investigate the IP addresses on your computer, there is a utility in the Windows directory called **Winipcfg.exe** which allows you to find out more. You can use **Winipcfg.exe** to check the IP address of any of your machines connected to the Internet, not just one running Internet Connection Sharing.

With your network up and running and your computers connected to the Internet, launch **Winipcfg.exe** from **Start** and **Run**.

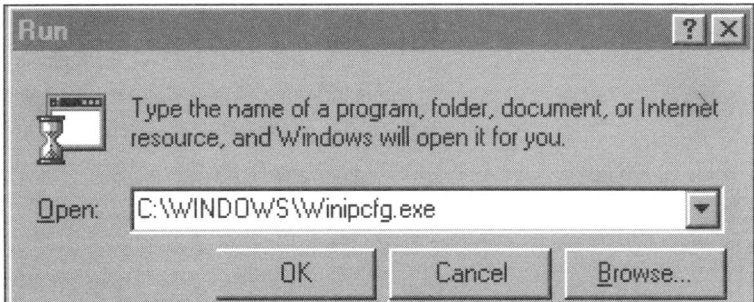

The **IP Configuration** window on the next page shows the result of running **Winipcfg.exe** on my Client machine Merlin, which is connected to my Gateway machine Kestrel, via a local area network.

You can see that the **IP Address** of the Client machine is **192.168.0.2**. The **Default Gateway** and **DHCP Server** are both set at **192.168.0.1**. This refers to the Gateway machine, in my case named Kestrel. Internet Connection Sharing uses these IP addresses as standard, i.e. **192.168.0.1** for the Gateway and **192.168.0.xx** for the Client machines.

If you want to change the IP address, for security reasons perhaps, highlight the address then select **Release** and **Renew**.

The above addresses are those allocated to a Client computer by the Internet Connection Sharing Gateway computer. The IP address applies to the network adapter fitted to a Client machine and remains constant on a given computer when running Internet Connection Sharing. If you run **Winipcfg.exe** on a machine connected directly to the Internet via a modem, using dynamic addressing the IP addresses will change every time an Internet connection is made.

Summary: Internet Connection Sharing

- Internet Connection Sharing enables two or more computers to browse the Internet over a single modem and telephone line.

- Internet Connection Sharing is a software component of Windows 98 Second Edition available as a low-cost upgrade CD or as a complete package.

- The computer fitted with the modem acts as a Gateway, handling requests for Internet information and routing back the answers.

- The computers on which users browse the Internet are known as Clients and these must be connected to each other and to the Gateway machine by a Local Area Network.

- All computers must have the Internet protocol TCP/IP, a component of Windows 98, installed from Windows Setup.

- Client machines are identified on the network by a unique IP (Internet Protocol) address of the form **192.168.0.253**. This is allocated by the Gateway machine and enables the forwarding of requests from browsers and the subsequent return of Internet information.

- Internet Connection Sharing must be installed from the Windows 98 Second Edition CD using Windows Setup.

- Setting up the Gateway machine is automated by a wizard and includes the preparation of a **Client Configuration Disk**. This floppy disc simplifies the setting up of each Client machine, including connection to the Internet across a LAN rather than directly via a modem.

- All dialling and direct connection to the Internet is handled via the Gateway machine, but users of Client machines can launch and use their browsers as if their machine had its own modem attached.

- The utility **C:\WINDOWS\Winipcfg.exe** allows IP addresses to be examined and changed if required.

Networking with Traveling LapLink

Introduction

Windows 98 provides a number of features for networking computers as discussed in previous chapters. These include the ability to create a peer-to-peer network and the **Direct Cable Connection** for connecting two machines by their serial or parallel ports. Also **Dial-Up Networking** which allows machines to be connected using modems. One of the main reasons for networking computers is to enable files to be copied between machines. For example, users of portable computers who spend time working away from their office-based desktop machine. A vast amount of data may accumulate and the files will need transferring to the office machine as quickly as possible. This may be done from a laptop in a remote location via the telephone network to the office. Alternatively the transfer could be done on returning to the office using a short cable (about 2 or 3 metres long) to connect the two machines.

While the networking features built into Windows 98 are perfectly adequate for many purposes, there are some very useful third party software packages which provide additional facilities. As described later, these include enhanced **File Transfer**, **Remote Control** of distant computers and **Print Redirection** (printing involving remote computers). LapLink Professional from Traveling Software, Inc and pcANYWHERE from SYMANTEC are two of the leading packages in this area of computing.

If you need to connect two machines which aren't on a peer-to-peer or client/server network or fitted with modems, packages like LapLink and pcANYWHERE include a serial or parallel cable.

So you can make a simple network using the cable provided to link two machines in close proximity (typically 2 or 3 metres apart).

My first experience of Traveling LapLink was as an essential tool used by computing professionals for copying large quantities of files between two standalone machines (as an alternative to endlessly swapping floppy discs). A typical situation would be when an office computer was replaced, posing the problem of how to transfer hundreds of files from the old machine to the new. The solution was simple - connect the two machines by a LapLink cable via their serial or parallel ports and install the LapLink software on both machines. It was then just a case of selecting some or all of the files and starting the copy process.

In its current version, LapLink Professional, the package still comes with a serial cable to carry out the basic task of copying between two standalone machines. However, LapLink Professional nowadays has a much wider range of services for use with computers linked by a variety of connection methods. Apart from the short cable linking serial, parallel or the latest ultra fast USB ports, they may be connected remotely via modems, Dial-Up Networking and the Internet. Alternatively they may be workstations on a local area network such as the peer-to-peer network described earlier.

For laptop machines fitted with *infrared* ports, a **Wireless** connection may be made with other machines fitted with an infrared device.   Computers using an ISDN adapter rather than a modem, should show an additional option **CAPI 2.0/ISDN** on the **Connect over** menu shown above. This Laplink connection method is used in a similar way to the modem connection described later in this chapter.

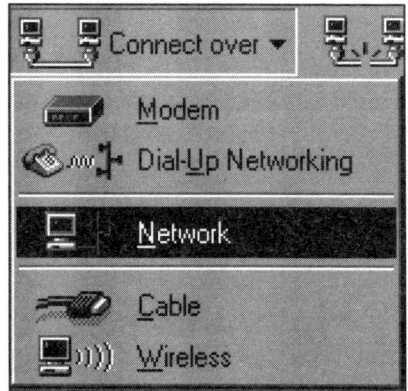

LapLink Professional

The software can be purchased on CD together with an instruction manual and a serial cable, from Traveling Software, or from the usual suppliers. Parallel cables and USB cables can be bought separately. You can also obtain a free Trial Version of the software on CD or download an evaluation copy from the Web site at :

www.travsoft.com

Downloading software from a Web site and installing on your hard disc is simply a matter of following the on-screen instructions. This topic is described earlier in this book for the trial version of iShare 3.0.

Installation of LapLink Professional from the CD starts automatically when you put the CD in the drive. You need to enter the serial number found on the CD case and there is a choice of an **Express** installation which includes all the common options or **Custom** installation which allows you to select the options to install. Then the files are copied from the CD to your hard disc and you are given the opportunity to set up **Print Redirection** either immediately or later.

After restarting the computer, LapLink Professional can be launched from the **Programs** menu off **Start**. When you first run LapLink Professional you are presented with the main window with the **LinkBar** across the top.

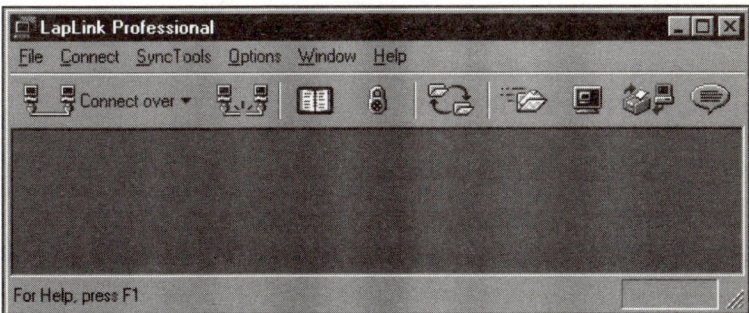

Security Options

No one can make a LapLink connection until suitable security options have been set. These are accessed by clicking on the padlock icon on the **LinkBar**.

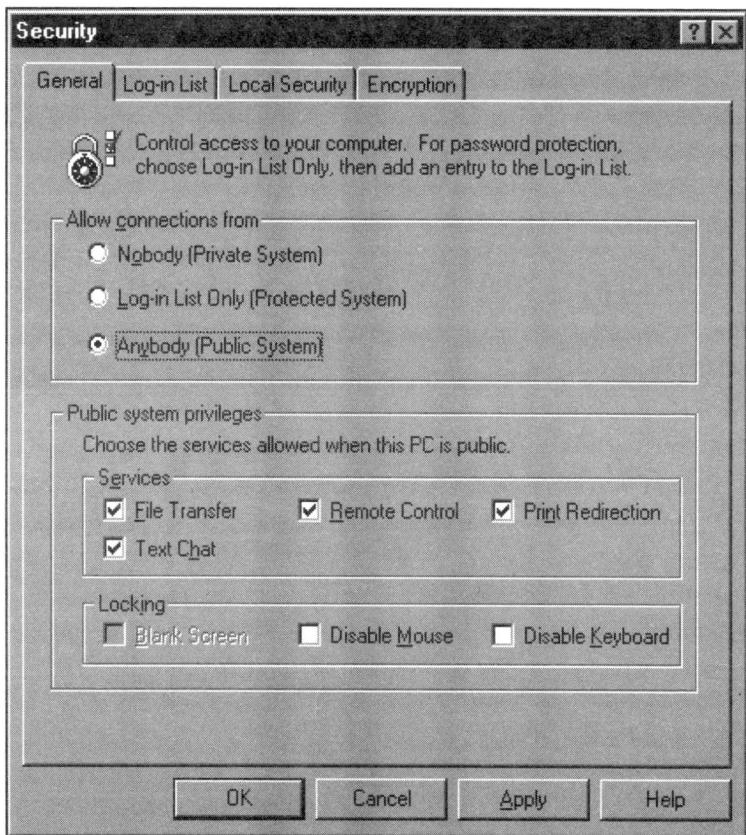

Nobody (Private System) - you can connect out to other machines, but no one can connect to yours.

Log-in List Only (Protected System) - you compile a list of log-in names and passwords for people allowed to connect to your machine (and potentially copy or delete files and alter settings).

When adding users to the Log-in List you can control which of the services (**File Transfer**, **Remote Control**, **Print Redirection** and **Text Chat**) they will be allowed to use.

Anybody (Public System) - With this security option set, anyone can connect to your machine so you should only switch on those services (**File Transfer**, **Remote Control**, **Print Redirection**, **Text Chat**) which you are happy for them to use.

The **Locking** options, when switched on, allow someone calling into the computer to blank the screen and disable the mouse and keyboard. If you want to work on a host, i.e. remote computer, you could arrange for the **Locking** options to be enabled on the host so that you could prevent other people using the keyboard or looking at the work you are doing.

LapLink Connections

Once the security options have been set, you are ready to make a connection to another computer. *Both machines must have LapLink running before you try to connect.* From the connection icon, select the method you wish to use.

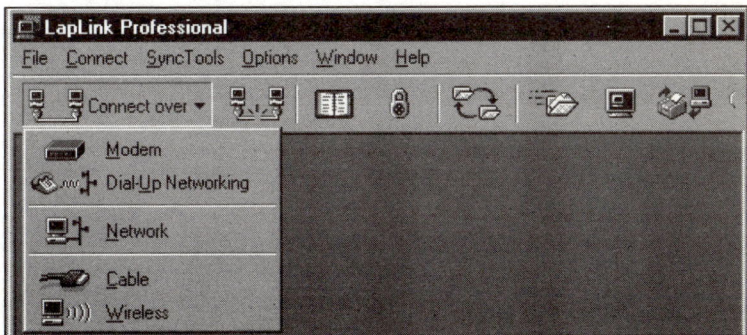

Cable Connections

Two local stand-alone machines (about 2 or 3 metres apart) can be connected using the **Cable** option, with either a serial, parallel or USB cable as supplied with LapLink or available from computer stores. This method would be useful, for example, when you brought a laptop in from your travels or had two standalone machines between which you want to transfer a substantial amount of data. The parallel cable will give better performance (faster data transfer) than the serial cable, but the USB cable far outperforms both. To avoid having to disconnect devices such as mice, printers and scanners to free up ports, it's worth considering the fitting of additional serial or parallel ports.

Before making the connection you need to set up the port you are going to use. If using a serial cable select COM1 or COM2, etc., or LPT1 or LPT2, etc., in the case of a parallel cable. (A USB connection is shown). Also tick **Enable Port**.

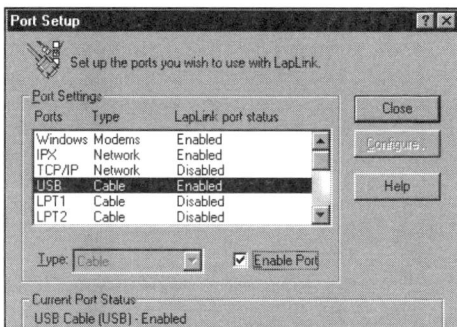

Once you have set up the ports on each machine and LapLink is running on both, your computer should detect the available connection, in this example a parallel cable on port LPT1 connecting to my remote computer called Merlin.

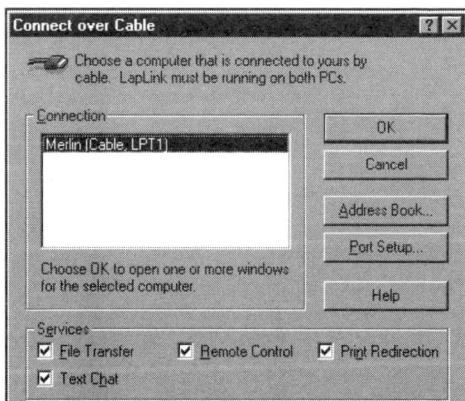

Now select with a tick the services which you wish to use (**File Transfer**, **Remote Control**, etc.). Click **OK** and the machines should beep to announce that the connection has been made and LapLink is now ready to run the selected services (discussed later).

Network Connections

Using Windows 98 on a peer-to-peer or client/server network you can copy files between workstations and also set up a shared printer, as described earlier. However, it's still worth installing LapLink Professional for the additional features it offers such as enhanced display of the folders for the two machines in windows side-by-side. Also the *synchronization* of files and automated scheduled copying using **Xchange Agent**. You can also remotely control another machine on the network for the purpose of using its files and software, carrying out maintenance or training and support of a person sitting at the remote machine.

Let's now consider setting up LapLink to work over a local area network such as the small peer-to-peer network discussed earlier which you might have in your home or small business. LapLink Professional doesn't work with the NetBEUI protocol recommended in the section on peer-to-peer networking. However, there are two more protocols in Windows 98, TCP/IP and IPX, which will work with LapLink. IPX is very much the faster for file transfer across a peer-to-peer network. If using IPX for the connection then you also need to ensure that Client for Microsoft Networks is installed.

No other setting up is required to run LapLink Professional across your network. You just need to ensure that the above components are included in the list obtained by selecting   **Start**, **Settings**, **Control Panel,** double-clicking the **Network** icon, and opening the **Network** dialogue box at the **Configuration** tab.

If any of the required components - the protocols **TCP/IP** and **IPX** and the **Client for Microsoft Networks** are not installed, click the **Add** button and select the required Microsoft components. You will need to have your Windows 98 CD available.

A more detailed description of the method for adding network components was given in the chapter **Windows 98 Networking** earlier in this book.

Once the correct components are installed, with LapLink Professional running, select **Connect over** and **Network**. Ensure that the network port(s) are enabled in **Port Setup...**, then click **Close**.

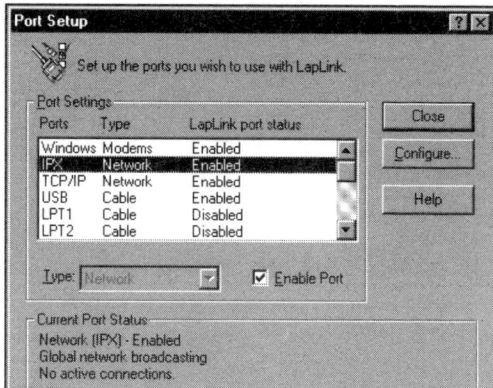

LapLink detects any connections which are available and displays them ready for you to make a selection. In this example, network connections are available to Richard's Desktop using either **IPX** or **TCP/IP** protocol. At this stage you also select the services (**File Transfer**, etc.) to be used in the session. After you have made your selections

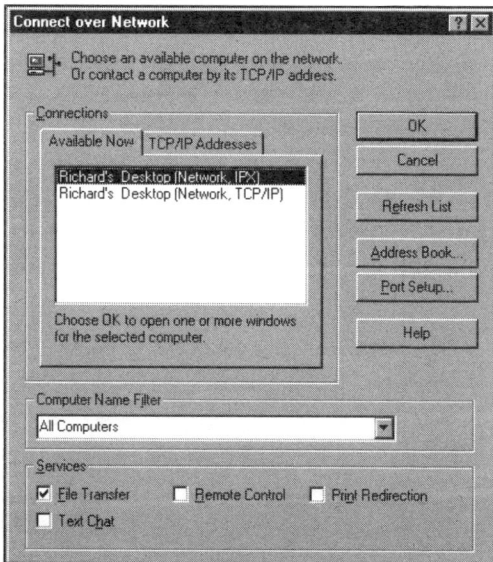

click **OK**. The connection is made and the guest computer beeps as windows open for each of the selected services.

Modem Connections

If your computer has a modem set up you can make a LapLink connection to another computer equipped with a modem by simply entering the telephone number of the computer you wish to connect to.

When you select **Connect over** and **Modem** the window on the right appears.

If you have previously entered the details of remote computers in the LapLink **Address Book**, their names will appear in a connection list under **Manual Dial**. Selecting one of the computers will place its telephone number in the **Phone Number** slot - otherwise you will have to enter the number manually.

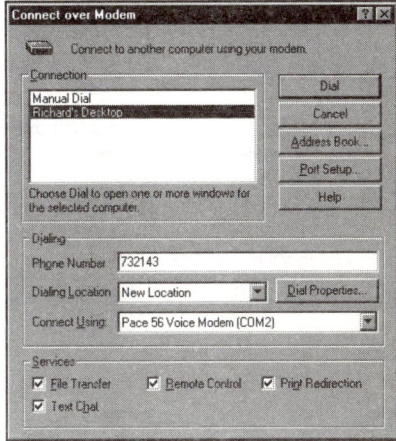

Clicking **Dial** brings up the **Dialing Status** window while your computer makes the connection with the remote machine. Then LapLink should open the windows for the services you have selected. (**File Transfer,** etc.) The machine which is being connected to may emit a beep as the connection is made. This may be switched off in LapLink in **Options**, **Connect Options...**, **Connect**.

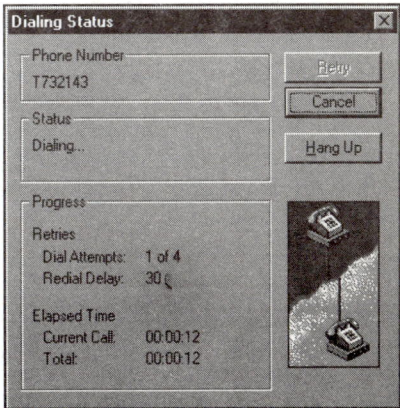

Dial-Up Networking

This is a component within Windows 98 and enables a computer with a modem to connect to another computer which is set up as a *network server*, such as the server of your Internet Service Provider. Selecting **Dial-Up Networking** within LapLink allows your computer to dial-up a server and access another machine which is running LapLink on the network .

Dial-up Networking may be used to enable someone out on the road or at home, to connect to their company network. This will probably require the collaboration of the Network Administrator in order to comply with security and technical considerations.

The Address Book

To automate future connections to a remote computer, click **Address Book...** and **Add** and add the **Descripton:**, **Computer Name:**, **Connection Type:** and **Telephone Number:** (if applicable), etc. You also need to select the **Services:** required and whether you want to blank the screen and disable the mouse and keyboard of the host machine. If you have been given a log-in name and password by the owner of the host machine these should also be entered in the **Address Book**.

Using LapLink Professional

Whichever connection method you are using to connect guest and host machines, the basic services (**File Transfer**, **Remote Control**, **Print Redirection** and **Text Chat**) are the same. Obviously operations such as transferring very large folders between machines will be faster on devices such as the peer-to-peer network and the USB cable than over a serial cable or a telephone line.

All operations are controlled from the **LinkBar** across the top of the LapLink window.

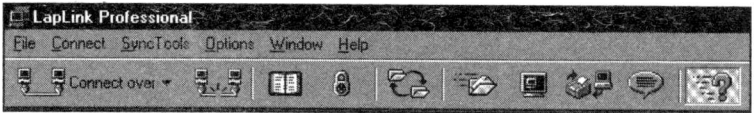

Before you click **OK** to make your selected connection you should ensure that you have chosen the LapLink services you will need during the session which is about to start.

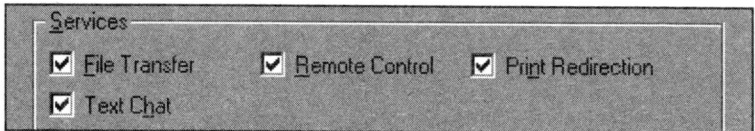

The next section gives an overview of the main LapLink services.

File Transfer

The file transfer service would typically be used by someone returning to their office (or connecting remotely), having accumulated a lot of new information on a laptop during their travels or when working at home.

Clicking on the **File Transfer** icon opens up Explorer-like windows for the two machines displayed side-by-side with their names across the top of their respective windows.

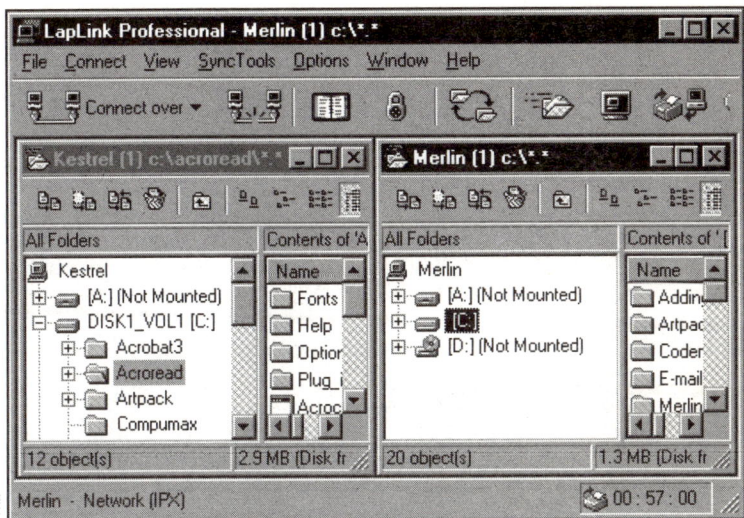

Copying can be achieved by dragging and dropping the required folders and files. Simultaneously holding down **CTRL** during the drag operation ensures that files are *copied*, while holding down **SHIFT** has the effect of *moving* files. Alternatively the **File** menu contains a full range of options which include copying, moving, deleting and renaming selected files and folders.

By default the **SpeedSync** feature is switched on. This ensures that whenever files are transferred from a source folder to a target folder of the same name on the other machine, only the data which has changed is transferred. There is also a **Clone Folder** tool which makes sure that source and target folders are identical. This includes removing from the target folder any files which do not exist in the source. Older versions of files in the target folder are overwritten by newer copies from the source.

Xchange Agent

This icon opens an **Xchange Agent**, also accessible from the **SyncTools** drop down menu on the **LinkBar**.

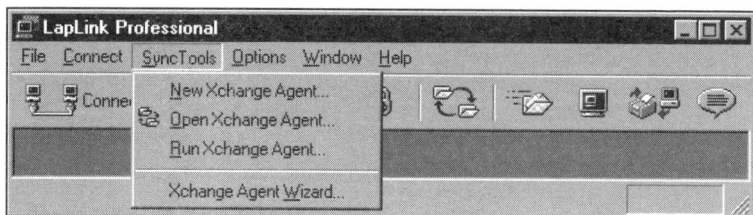

An Xchange Agent is an automated copying operation between two computers running LapLink. This can be saved and run manually when required or at a scheduled time. Synchronization ensures that corresponding folders on both machines have the latest versions of files. A preview feature allows you to confirm that the scheduled operation is what you really want to do.

Remote Control

When you click this icon from the **LinkBar**, the desktop of the remote machine appears on your screen. This gives you complete control of the remote machine, using your mouse and keyboard, just as if you were sitting in front of the remote machine. This enables you to carry out management and maintenance tasks on the remote machine. Or you might wish to look at the e-mail on your desktop machine back at the office while you're using your laptop from a hotel room in some remote part of the world. You can also re-boot the host machine, for example to effect any changes you have made to the setup. If you don't want anyone to use the remote (or host) machine or look at the work you are doing on it, there are options which enable you to lock the host keyboard and mouse and blank the screen.

While you are working at your machine (the guest), a person can sit at the remote (host) machine and both of you can alternately operate the host machine. This would, for example, allow you to collaborate on a joint document in Word or some other Windows application. Alternatively you could carry out interactive training and support with the person sitting at the remote machine. Since the connection might be over a telephone line, a local network or the Internet, the **Remote Control** feature of LapLink offers considerable potential for savings in travel to customers' or colleagues' work places.

Print Redirection

This service allows you to use printers attached to remote computers, for example because they offer colour or higher quality than any printers available locally. So you could prepare a document on your computer at home or out on your travels, then while still away from base, use Print Redirection to produce high quality output on the machine back at the office. Alternatively if you are away from your main place of work you might need a copy of a particular document stored on the office machine. You can use Print Redirection to retrieve the document from the remote machine and print out a copy on a printer attached to your local machine. So Print Redirection allows you to print documents on printers attached to computers at either end of a LapLink connection.

Before you can print using a printer attached to a remote (host) machine, you must have your local (guest) machine set up with the printer software just as if the printer were attached to the local machine. To start this process, select **Options** and **Print Redirection Options...** from the LinkBar in LapLink Professional. Then select **Setup...** as shown right. For this you will need to have your Windows CD or the driver discs provided by the manufacturer of the printer. Once you have made a connection, you

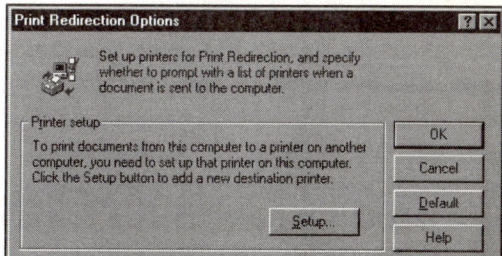

simply run the application and open the document to be printed. Then using the standard **File/Print** command in the application you select, from the list of available printers, the required printer (it should have **LapLink** after its name).

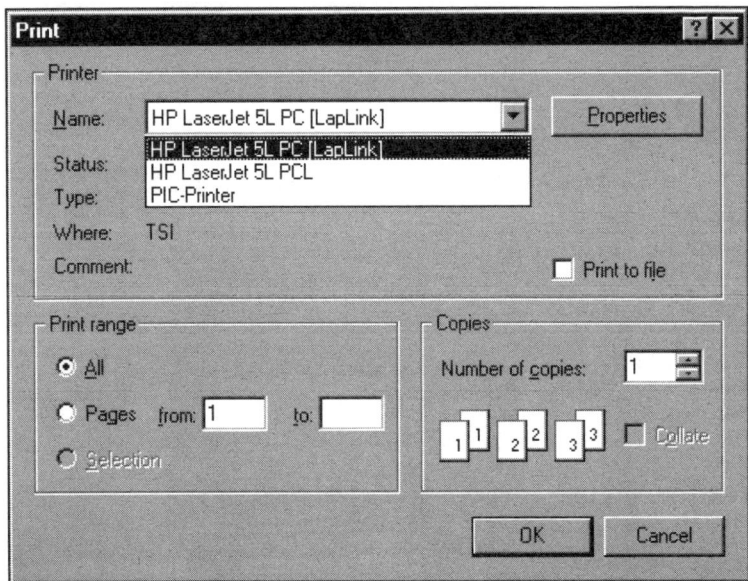

Text Chat

This service allows you to send short messages to a colleague running LapLink on a remote machine. **Text Chat** could be used, for example, while giving support or training to someone using modems over the only available telephone line - so that no other method of two-way communication is possible. Ensure that **Text Chat** is ticked when you make the connection.

```
LapLink Professional - Richard's Desktop - Text Chat    _ □ ×
File   Edit   Connect   SyncTools   Options   Window   Help

  Connect over ▼

  Richard's Desktop - Text Chat                    _ □ ×

   ---------- David's Laptop ----------
   How's the new project coming along ?

   ---------- Richard's Desktop ----------
   I'm making progress. I've been to see the customer and agreed  the
   specification.

   OK. Let me know if there are any problems.

  Richard's Desktop  - Network [IPX]              00 : 05 : 18
```

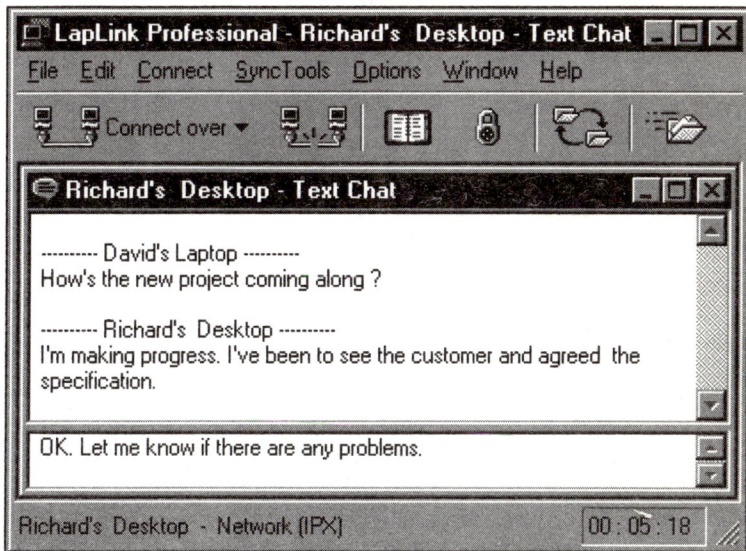

Text is typed in the lower panel, then sent when you press **Enter**. The **Text Chat** window will pop up in the foreground of the remote machine, displaying your message. Your messages and the replies appear in the top panel of your computer, under the names of the computers they were sent from.

Messages can be prepared offline in advance of making a Laplink connection using a Windows 98 application like **Notepad.** Then it is copied to the clipboard using the **Copy** command in the Windows application. After the connection has been made, use **Edit** and **Paste** in **Text Chat** to place the text into the bottom panel in the **Text Chat** window. In a similar fashion text can be copied from **Text Chat** into another Windows application.

Summary: Networking with Traveling LapLink

- Traveling LapLink provides a range of services between computers which have been connected locally via a short cable or local area network and remotely via a modem/ISDN and the telephone lines.

- File transfer using a USB cable connection is very much faster than with a cable connecting parallel ports, which in turn is faster than the serial cable.   IPX provides very fast network file transfers   while similar operations over telephone lines are relatively slow.

- LapLink Professional has many additional features designed to enable mobile laptop computer users to communicate with their desktop machines and office networks. Equally to enable the home user to communicate with their work computers or those of friends and colleagues in distant locations.   Apart from File Transfer, these features include Remote Control, Print Redirection and Text Chat.

- Remote Control allows the user to take over a distant computer and use and manage the machine just as if he or she were sitting in front of it. This enables training and support at the remote machine.

- Print Redirection enables documents to be retrieved from remote computers and printed locally.   Alternatively documents stored on a local computer may be output on a remote printer when there is no suitable printer available locally.

- Text Chat is used to send and receive messages during a LapLink session such as training or online support.

- Xchange Agent allows the scheduling of file transfers and *synchronization* ensures that folders contain the latest files.

- Speedsync saves time by only copying the changed parts of files.

- Security features built into LapLink include an option to prevent unauthorised access to a computer. Access to the LapLink services (File Transfer, Remote Control, etc.) can also be controlled.

Appendix A: The Universal Serial Bus

Your computer(s), if they are of recent design (later Pentiums) may already be fitted with USB ports. To make sure, look at the back of the machine near to the connectors for devices such as the mouse and printer, etc. The USB ports are small rectangular slots about 12mm by 5mm.

If your machine doesn't already have any visible USB ports, all is not lost - it should be possible to fit the connectors at a modest cost. The basic requirement is for a Pentium or equivalent computer running Windows 98. If no USB ports are visible externally, it's still possible that your computer is equipped with USB ports on the motherboard but simply requires a cable and backplate to provide a connector on the back of the machine. In this case a USB backplate can be bought for a few pounds from local specialist computer suppliers or by mail order from companies such as Maplins.

Even if your machine is supplied with USB ports you still need to check that USB is **enabled** in the BIOS settings of your computer. The BIOS is usually entered as your machine is starting up, by responding to a message on the screen such as "**Press DEL to enter SETUP**".

If you have an early Pentium there may be no USB support at all on the motherboard. You can overcome this by fitting a USB PCI Adapter Card. This is an expansion card which plugs into the motherboard and provides two USB connectors on the back of the machine. Before buying a USB Adapter Card you should remove the cover of your computer and check there is a vacant (white) PCI slot, not to be confused with the longer (black) ISA slots.

A number of major companies involved with USB technology have set up a USB Web site containing useful information. You can find the site on the Internet at:

www.usb.org

Apart from news about peripheral devices designed to utilise the latest USB technology, it's also possible to download a piece of software called **USBREADY.EXE**. This examines your system and reports on the level of USB support which your system provides.

When you run the testing software, if your machine is already equipped for USB, a message will be displayed saying "**This system has FULL support for USB.**" (You may still need a cable and ports on a backplate to provide the connections on the outside of the machine). One of my computers had the USB pins already in place on the motherboard - it just needed a cheap ATX Form Card to be plugged in. This gave two USB sockets and two PS/2 mouse sockets on the back of the machine. The manual for your computer's motherboard should give precise details of what connectors are available.

However, if you are unlucky, (as I was with my older machine) the USB testing software will display the following result:

In this case you will need to fit a USB PCI Adapter Card as described in the next section. These can be bought for under £20 from local computer repair/upgrade specialists.

Fitting a USB Adapter Card

This section assumes you have checked there is a spare white PCI slot available in your computer and you have obtained a suitable USB Adapter Card.

Switch your computer off at the power point but leave the power cable plugged in at the wall. From time to time while working, earth yourself by touching the metal chassis of the computer. Remove the casing of your computer, usually by taking out several screws at the back or side of the machine. Remove the blanking plate adjacent to a spare PCI slot and firmly press the USB Adapter into place. Fit the card retaining screw, replace the computer casing and restart the machine.

As PCI expansion cards should be truly "Plug and Play" compatible, all being well you will see a message announcing that new hardware has been found.

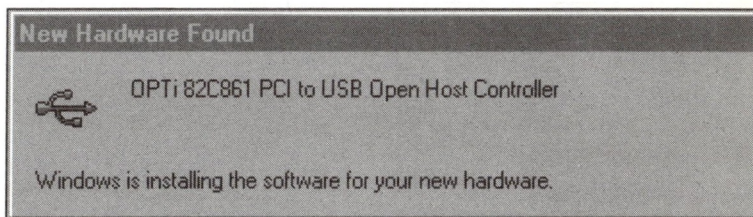

Then you are asked to insert the Windows 98 CD so that the necessary software can be installed.

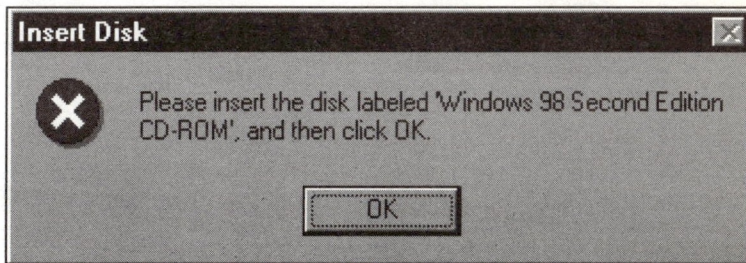

After the software has been copied, your new USB ports should be ready for use. You can check this by looking in the **Device Manager** obtained by selecting **Start**, **Settings**, **Control Panel** and double clicking **System**. Select the **Device Manager** tab and then **Universal Serial Bus controllers**. You should see the name of the USB Adapter displayed, in this case the **OPTi** model, as shown below.

The USB port should now be ready to use. (A fault with the device would be indicated by an exclamation mark in a yellow circle). You will need to obtain a suitable cable before you can use the new USB ports to link two computers for data transfer work. You can buy these for LapLink from the Web site of Traveling Software at **www.travsoft.com**.

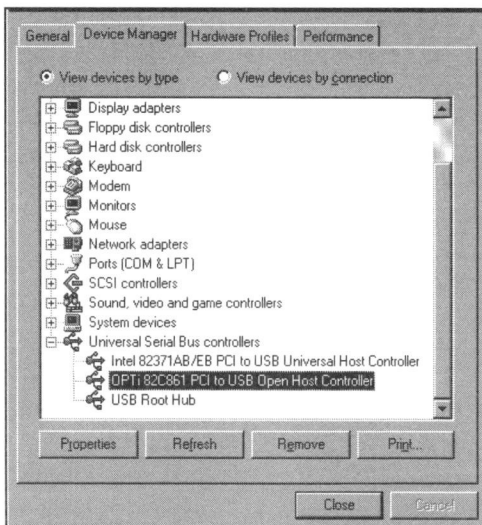

The cable package also includes a floppy disc containing the LapLink USB driver. This must be installed on both of the computers to be connected. Windows 98 detects the new cable and you simply insert the floppy disc giving **Drive A:** as the location of the software for the new device.

At the time of writing it appears that LapLink Professional is the first of the popular data transfer programs to embrace the high speed USB technology.

Appendix B: Fitting a Parallel Port Expansion Card

The parallel port is a 25-way female socket on the back of the computer, commonly referred to as the Printer Port and LPT1. By design the parallel port is much faster than the neighbouring serial port. Consequently the parallel port is favoured by manufacturers of scanners, Zip drives and data transfer software and cables, apart from its primary function as a printer port.

Unfortunately, although it's technically possible to have more than one device sharing a single parallel port, this does not give optimum performance. Also, for data transfer work between computers with a program like the Direct Cable Connection or LapLink Professional, you will probably need to disconnect any other devices already using the port. Clearly if you want to use a parallel link on a regular basis - say to back up your laptop computer onto a desktop machine, it's very inconvenient to have to keep disconnecting printers and other devices. The only solution is to fit one or more extra parallel ports to each machine as required. (Up to 4 parallel ports designated LPT1-LPT4 may be fitted to a modern PC).

Extra parallel ports can be bought on expansion cards which plug into slots on the *motherboard*, the main printed circuit board inside of your computer. Cards designed for the older ISA standard are cheaper than the newer PCI standard. The ISA cards fit into long black slots on the motherboard while the PCI slots are white and shorter. Before buying any expansion card you should check that you have a spare slot of the right type on the motherboard. Expansion cards are available from computer dealers and mail order companies such as Maplins.

If you can afford a PCI card it will be easier to set up under Windows 98 than an ISA card. The procedure is similar to that for a USB Adapter as described in Appendix A. It's just a case of removing the case of the computer and inserting the card in a vacant PCI slot. Then when you restart the computer Windows 98 should automatically detect the new hardware and complete the installation.

The cheaper ISA card is harder to install since it's not Plug and Play compatible. First you need to set some jumpers on the card to match the available IRQs in your computer. These are the Interrupt Request settings, numbered 0-15 and refer to lines of communication between the device and the central processor of the computer. Two devices can share the same IRQ number but only if they will not be used simultaneously. First you need to find the available IRQs by looking at **Start**, **Settings**, **Control Panel**, **System**, **Device Manager** and **Computer**. Some IRQs which appear to be available may in fact be reserved for use by the system.

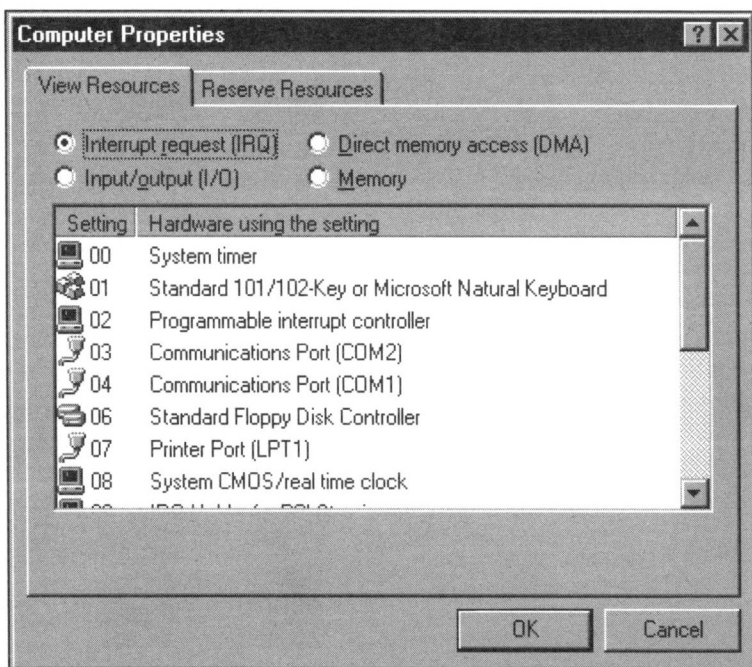

You can see from the above that IRQ7 is used for the first parallel port LPT1. Fortunately IRQ5 is not listed above, so this is available for our new parallel port LPT2. (IRQ5 is commonly used for a second parallel port).

Now look at the instructions supplied with the parallel port expansion card and locate the *jumpers*. These are small push-on connectors used to bridge pairs of pins on the card.

The instructions should explain how to set the jumpers to give the appropriate IRQ number (IRQ5 or whatever). Next, with your computer switched off, remove the case and carefully but firmly insert the parallel port expansion card in an available ISA slot. Then replace the retaining screw which secures the card to the chassis and fit the case to the computer. When you restart the computer the parallel port should be detected and assigned the name LPT2. (If the ISA card is not detected automatically you will have to run the **Add New Hardware** applet accessed from **Start**, **Settings** and **Control Panel**).

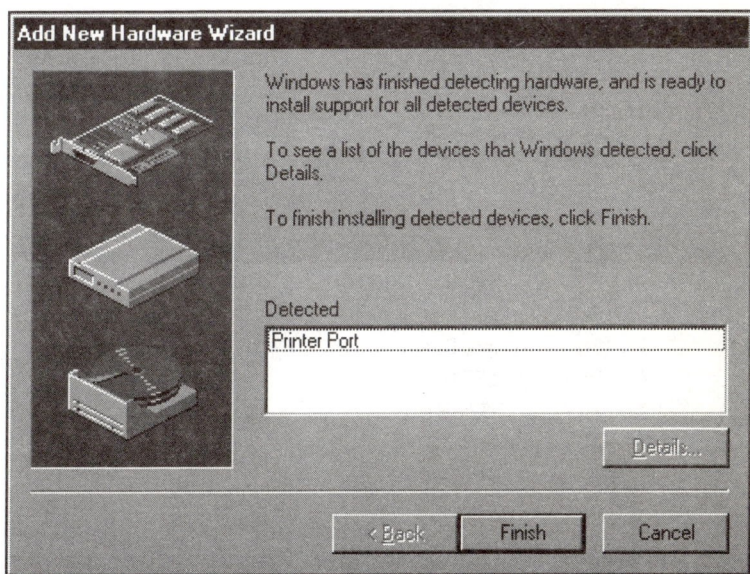

Now click **Finish** to complete the installation. You can check if the port has been installed by looking for LPT2 in the list of ports in the **Device Manager** (**Start**, **Settings**, **Control Panel and System**).

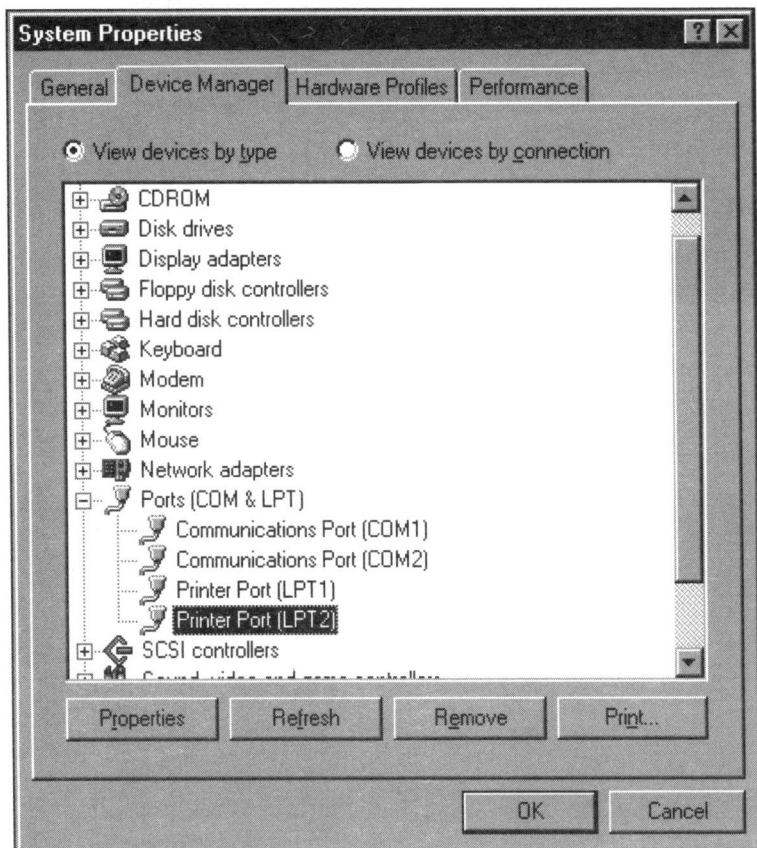

Any problems with the card are likely to be with the Interrupt Setting or possibly because the card itself has not been properly seated in the ISA slot on the motherboard.

You can examine the interrupt settings in Windows 98 by double clicking on **LPT2** in the **Device Manager** then selecting **Resources**.

To make changes you need to remove the tick from **Use Automatic Settings** then select **Change Setting...**.

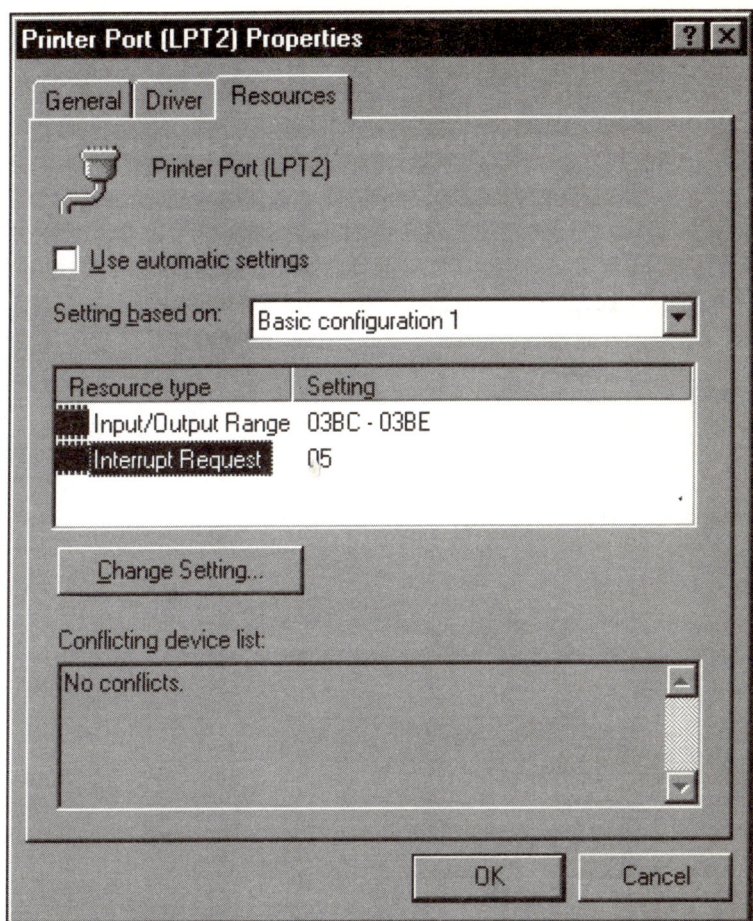

Printer Port (LPT2) Properties

General | Driver | **Resources**

Printer Port (LPT2)

☐ Use automatic settings

Setting based on: | Basic configuration 1 |▼|

Resource type	Setting
Input/Output Range	03BC - 03BE
Interrupt Request	05

Change Setting...

Conflicting device list:

No conflicts.

OK | Cancel

You may need to experiment with the **Basic Configuration** by scrolling down in the **Setting Based on:** bar. You should highlight each of the settings **Input/Output Range** and **Interrupt Request** in turn and check that **No Conflicts** appears in the panel under **Conflicting device list:**. Any alterations you make to the above software settings in Windows 98 must correspond to the physical jumper settings on the expansion card. Typical settings for LPT2 are **IRQ5** and **0278-027A** for the **Input/Output Range** although a different value had to be set in the above example.

Notes

Index